A PERFECT

STORM

HOW TO THRIVE IN AN UNCERTAIN AND EVER-CHANGING WORLD

MICHAEL TOBIN OBE

K
N
O
W
N

WWW.GET-KNOWN.CO.UK

"I've had undeterred and resolute belief over the years that there is no such thing as 'work-life balance', it has to be 'work-life integration'. Unfortunately, it took the pandemic to bring this realisation to life for many, as they begin to experience the joy, bliss, and success of true work-life integration, and I am living testament of that – one who has not only believed in this, but has lived it as well!"

— Michael Tobin, OBE

ABOUT THE AUTHOR

Born in the backstreets of Bermondsey, serial technology entrepreneur Michael Tobin OBE is known as the 'Maverick'[1] for his unconventional management style, like the time he took his team swimming with sharks to teach them how to manage their fear. Today, he is widely credited with having been *'instrumental in creating the digital infrastructure of the Internet of Europe'* (Lord Vaizey MP).

In 2014 he was recognised by Her Majesty the Queen with an OBE for Services to the Digital Economy, following his unwavering dedication to the datacentre industry. His day at the Palace was a long way from his humble childhood beginnings that included suffering periods of homelessness, violence, and dodging petrol bombs in Rhodesia.

Michael's outstanding achievements earned him many awards during his career including: 'Datacentre and Cloud Influencer of the Decade' (Broadgroup Industry Awards), 'Top 25 Power Individuals of Industry' (Smith and Williamson), 'UK IT Services Entrepreneur of the Year' (Ernst & Young) three years running, and 'Lifetime Achievement for Services to the Data Centre Industry' (Data Centre Europe Awards).

Today, Michael works around the clock in his Non-Exec Director and Chairman roles and undertakes charity missions that continue to test his limits. His latest missions to support and empower young and vulnerable people have included sleeping in the streets for homeless charities, running 40 marathons in 40 days for the Prince's Trust, and in January 2020 undertaking a challenging and dangerous trek to the South Pole, supporting The Brain Tumour Charity to beat brain tumours in children.

DEDICATION

"Fate whispers to the warrior,
'You cannot withstand the storm.'
The warrior whispers back,
'I am the storm.'"

UNKNOWN

So much of my strength comes from others… whether
that's colleagues, friends, or family. Regardless of how
invincible we believe we are, ultimately everyone needs
support. My lighthouse in every storm is my wonderful
and beautiful wife, Shalina. Thank you x

Eloise, Nelson and Rose, you continue to fill me with
pride as you grow into adulthood. You are a constant
source of inspiration. Thank you x

CONTENTS

INTRODUCTION

Perfect Storm (noun) [singular]: *'an occasion when several bad things happen at the same time, creating a situation that could not be worse'*

OXFORD ENGLISH DICTIONARY[2]

THE CALM BEFORE THE STORM

On 23rd March 2020, in the 75th year since our nation celebrated the end of World War II, Britain went into lockdown. In a televised speech to the nation, then Prime Minister Boris Johnson calmly but firmly ordered the British people to 'Stay at home, protect our NHS and save lives'.[3] If this was the calm before the storm, it didn't take long for the wind to start howling and the rain to pour down.

All schools, non-essential shops and businesses, pubs, restaurants, libraries, playgrounds, leisure centres and churches were ordered to close until further notice. Overnight the streets fell silent and people watched from their windows in stunned silence while the country faced its biggest threat in decades. With police out on strict patrol, panic in the supermarket aisles and no live sport, or anything much else other than news and re-runs of classic soaps on the television for a while, we found ourselves at war again, but this time with an invisible killer, Covid-19.

Dr Tedros Adhanom Ghebreyesus, Director General, World Health Organisation, summed up the gravity of the situation when he said:

'This is the defining global health crisis of our time. The days, weeks and months ahead will be a test of our resolve, a test of our trust in science, and a test of solidarity.

'This amazing spirit of human solidarity must become even more infectious than the virus itself. Although we may have to be physically apart from each other for a while, we can come together in ways we never have before.'[4]

The Covid-19 virus allegedly emerged from an outdoor, live animal market in Wuhan in December 2019. Scientists suggested that the virus jumped from a bat onto another animal before being passed on to a human, where it spread in an alarmingly rapid chain reaction of coughs and sneezes, before the world, quite literally, caught on.

Many more conspiracy theories started to spread as quickly as the virus, from it being biological warfare leaked from a lab, or the technological consequences of 5G, but in any case, the brand-new virus sent scientists into a complete spin. Within a matter of weeks, the virus had spread to nearly every country and within months, millions of people had been affected with hundreds of thousands of infections and deaths recorded worldwide. We were officially in a global pandemic.

In a very short time, the Covid-19 crisis was taking thousands of lives daily. As we watched the death toll mounting, our only choice was to wait out the storm while the scientists developed a vaccine for a virus that was here to stay. Suddenly the world we lived in had changed forever, and we would have to change with it. In the words of Dr Tedros: 'The world will not and cannot go back to the way things were. There must be a "new normal" – a world that is healthier, safer and better prepared.'[5]

DARK CLOUDS LOOMING

Within days of the March lockdown announcement, the UK had joined the rest of the world and disappeared indoors to contain the spread of Covid-19. In the UK, the National Health Service focused on saving lives, and key workers including doctors, nurses, emergency services, supermarket workers, delivery drivers and care assistants, amongst others, mobilised to keep communities running. Social distancing rules meant people stayed a designated number of metres apart, whilst mentally pulling together to contain the greatest threat to our liberties in living memory.

While Covid-19 brought the world to its knees, Britain was also plunged into its deepest financial recession for more than 300 years, one that proved to be much worse than the Great Depression of the 1930s. If you combine the fallout from the dot-com bubble burst in 2000 with that of the global financial crisis in 2008 you might just be getting close to the massive fiscal fallout that began with Covid-19 and continues to rage on today. But now there were even more dark clouds looming, and another silent killer in our midst. Suicide.

The Covid pandemic restrictions meant that many people found themselves alone, without access to their families and friends, terrified for their loved ones, their jobs, their homes, their relationships and their futures. For many of the most vulnerable in society, the lack of access to mental health support had an instant impact on their health. There was another pandemic on the horizon, one that sadly I had become all too familiar with over the years. Men like me, whose identities were enveloped with their professional roles and aspirations, and who wanted to support their families and protect their loved ones, felt utterly lost, hopeless, and unable to reach out for help. Their struggle to survive the fallout of the virus led to a collective silence that was deafening, and they found themselves drifting on a new sea of sadness and despair.

Research conducted by The Royal College of Psychiatrists[6] shows that during financial downturns rates of suicide increase, and men are more at risk if they lose their job during a recession. According to the suicide prevention charity CALM, suicide remains the single biggest killer of men under 45 in the UK. Out of the 125 lives that are lost every week to suicide in the UK, 75% of these are male.[7]

We still don't know the data on how many more lives were taken due to the combined impact of the Covid pandemic, the inevitable recession and loss of jobs, but I do know that the impact was very real for many men in my life, including several close friends and colleagues, who tragically fell silent all too soon.

THE EYE OF THE STORM

There are times in all of our lives when we find ourselves in the eye of the storm. At this moment we feel so overwhelmed it's impossible to make out the clouds, let alone see any silver linings.

The last few years have certainly brought one storm after the other, with little respite. In fact, when Covid-19 arrived we thought that was the storm, and once it passed we'd be safe again. But really it was just the start of a stormy decade: from the pandemic to the financial crisis, Russia's war on Ukraine instigating a fuel and energy crisis, multiple political uprisings and reshuffles, three UK Prime Ministers in as many months, and the sudden loss of 'the rock on which modern Britain was built',[8] Her Majesty, Queen Elizabeth II. Not to mention having our own unique personal circumstances to deal with too; we have all felt overwhelmed at least once in the past few years. These storms have been enough to send even the most plucky of spirits into a complete downward spiral. But the related stress and devastating number of families who have been affected by the loss of lives through depression is overwhelming and a feeling of there being 'no way out' can no longer be accepted as the norm. Now we must act. We must speak up, reach out, and hold on, and we must do everything we can to change the ending of this all-too-common story, because no matter how severe the storm, life is always worth living.

STEP INTO THE LIGHT

"The shadow is the greatest teacher
for how to come to the light."

RAM DASS

This book is for anyone who has ever felt overwhelmed by life, but specifically for the young man that I once was, and who I still see in myself today. The highly functioning, ambitious individual with hopes and dreams that varied vastly, from just being able to buy enough food for another day, to paying the bills that month, right through to achieving that dream job, finding the perfect partner for life, and raising a family.

My somewhat unconventional approach to management over almost five decades of business springs from often very personal pain and toil. These experiences, however, have given me life lessons that have stuck with me and influenced the way I choose to operate. From homelessness and domestic violence as a child, to bitter business battles and blackmail as a business leader, to running multiple marathons and trekking through the most extreme conditions to reach the South Pole to raise vital funds for charity, these often extremely challenging, frightening and exhausting lessons have taught me determination, resilience and, above all, a true sense of survival.

My aim in this book is to inspire you to take the path to a happier, more adventurous life. Whatever your situation, no matter how impossible, hopeless and desperate things can feel, there is *always* a choice: to stick or twist, a choice between not taking action or making a change. There's a saying about how worrying is like a rocking chair: it gives you something to do but gets you nowhere. The value of worrying is negative. You can either do something to improve the potential outcome, or there is nothing you can do. Either way, sitting there worrying just causes more problems and often exacerbates the likelihood of the outcome to happen. So rather than sit in our chairs waiting for tomorrow to arrive, here's just a few ways in which we will work through this book and face some familiar issues together.

HOW TO EAT AN ELEPHANT

"There is only one way to eat an elephant:
one bite at a time."

DESMOND TUTU

Compartmentalisation is the act of organising your mountain of thoughts into much smaller molehills. When you have multiple things to deal with, it all feels so overwhelming, but if you break them down into separate bite-size chunks and tackle them one by one, it becomes more manageable. In other words, most battles in life that seem daunting, overwhelming, and even impossible, can be overcome gradually by taking them on just a little at a time. For a busy, always on-the-go person who finds it difficult to say no, learning how to divide everything up into actionable chunks has made all the difference for me and I will share reflections on my experiences so that this technique can make a difference to you too.

DON'T MAN UP, OPEN UP!

I've found enlightenment in some of the darkest moments in my life simply by talking to people about how I am feeling. Yes, sharing your innermost thoughts and feelings can feel uncomfortable or even just unfamiliar, but a problem shared really is a problem halved. The sooner you coax yourself to share how you feel, the easier it will become. It's time to move past the pride, shame and embarrassment and discover the actions that can be taken to deal with the issues. And don't be afraid to seek professional help as well as talking to friends, colleagues and family. In this book I recommend some truly valuable organisations and resources that you can investigate or get in touch with today if you need to. They are ready to listen and support you right now.

FINDING YOUR 45º

You might be finding that one of the major challenges of balancing work and life means that neither can be perfect – and the sooner we can accept that, the better. You might triumph on one axis, at 0°, but at the same time completely mess things up on the other axis, at 90°. For example, you can't be an Olympic gold-medal-winning weightlifter *and* an equally awarded marathon runner. Both disciplines require completely different sets of muscles. If you become champion of one, you will probably have to drop (or at least compromise on) the other, because it's unlikely you will win a gold medal for *both*. But instead, you could master the decathlon, which still calls upon your multiple strengths and skills, but it allows you to succeed at both as a 45° solution. You win gold, and you enjoy both your favourite disciplines!

Most of us find ourselves in an uphill struggle when we try to balance two or more competing demands, and I am no exception. I've experienced the dire consequences of spreading myself too thin. So now, rather than trying to be perfect at 0° *and* 90°, the ultimate goal is to aim for 100% success at 45°.

If we apply this refreshing new angle to our 'new normal', i.e. what life looks like since the pandemic and continuing crises, and in the future, it could provide the emotional and practical tools we need to identify our own equivalent of the 45° angle instead, and therefore allow us to adapt and create more sustainable levels of achievement and expectation in both our home and work lives. For me, 'home' and 'work' lives have never been different, they have been one. There is only one 'me', so I lead my life in an integrated fashion and I no longer feel the need to compromise home or work to achieve a so-called 'balance'. In this book I will share my experiences with you so that you can integrate life and work and find the perfect angle that works for you.

EVER-READINESS

When Covid-19 hit, it dawned on me that my life so far has been one huge exercise in disaster planning for something of this nature. Looking at how I live nowadays, I've been 'ever-ready' to thrive under virus conditions for decades, with tech enabling my life wherever it possibly can and helping me to survive lockdowns and the like. But I know I'm lucky to have embraced technology early in life and throughout my career in the data centre industry. It's not too late to harness whatever we can right now that will enable us to face whatever the future may hold – and there are some great ways to do this with the help of technology that I'll introduce in this book.

IT'S TIME TO DANCE IN THE RAIN

*"And once the storm is over, you won't remember how
you made it through, how you managed to survive. You
won't even be sure, whether the storm is really over.
But one thing is certain. When you come out of the
storm, you won't be the same person who walked in.
That's what this storm's all about."*

HARUKI MURAKAMI

This book offers an actionable guide to building inner strength and thriving in an uncertain and ever-changing world. Packed full of practical advice and tips that have helped me through the difficult times. I am not a professional in the area of mental health, but I am here to share some of my experiences to help you with yours. Even just one new technique, tool, or new habit can make your life feel a little bit easier to manage.

Exploring the common themes that impact on all our lives, from Finance to Health, Education to Culture, this book is designed to be digested in bite-size chunks. Through my reflections on the impact of the crisis on our daily lives and many of my own personal stories, each chapter reveals my personal advice and tips on how to integrate new technologies and techniques into your life that will help to find the most positive angle possible for you to stop being overwhelmed. In the end, you will be more empowered to LIVE life to the full, integrate your LOVE and WORK to reach your potential, and PROSPER whilst you navigate this ever-changing and increasingly uncertain world.

CHAPTER 1

TECHNOLOGY

"Lightning makes no sound until it strikes."

MARTIN LUTHER KING JR.

The pandemic turned out to be the first in a long line of fast and furious storms, which left us in no doubt that we are in a VUCA state – that is, facing a 'volatile, uncertain, complex and ambiguous' world.[9] In what felt like a lightning flash, the world changed and continues to change. In fact, it's been such a series of events that we coined the term 'permacrisis'[10] to describe how truly awful this period has been for so many people. There were too many dark sides during the pandemic, but as someone who has always believed technology can help us thrive rather than just survive, the bright side that stood out for me was that technology became our port in a storm.

This chapter is about how positively integrating technology into your life could lower your stress levels, improve your health and relationships and help you prosper in this uncertain, ever-changing and stormy world.

Live

DATA ON DEMAND

I've been riding on the waves of technology since an early age. From my apprenticeship at Rockwell Engineering at 16 to my role as CEO at Telecity Group, the FTSE 250 data centre operator I took from £6 million to £2.6 billion, to my many non-executive roles at companies across the globe – technology and its global digital infrastructure has underpinned every aspect of my life, including my health and wellbeing. But when I found myself working in the data centre industry almost 30 years ago, I had no idea how fundamental it would become to *everybody's* lives across the planet.

Data centres are where the Internet lives, and since Covid-19 they have become the lifeblood for everything we do. The wires lying beneath the floor tiles of the multi-billion-dollar global industry carry more web-traffic than the M25 carries cars on a Monday morning. They have the power to support billions of pounds' worth of business transactions every year – and to cause chaos if they fail. The subsea cables lying on the ocean floors connecting various continents and countries together, today support more than $10 trillion in daily commercial transactions.

Coping with the Covid-driven onslaught of demand for data in early 2020 was like Armageddon for the Internet and became the ultimate stress test for data centres. With mass movement online like never before as people leapt from their offline lives to online safety; demand for bandwidth almost outstripped supply as getting on the Internet became an essential human need, making it almost as hard to get hold of as toilet paper for a little while!

HEART ON YOUR SLEEVE

Data centres are also busy supporting the wealth of smart technology devices at our fingertips. I don't mean egg timers, hair brushes and talking fridges, but genuine digital solutions that help us achieve a higher quality of life, health and wellbeing.

I truly believe that smart wearables like fitness wristbands, watches and fashion accessories are paving the way for the next generation of health tools that exist outside of the doctor's office, ones that can harness data to provide valuable health insights and fast-track critical patient care. As a nation of Fitbit fanatics and app-oholics, we're well acquainted with tracking and logging our daily milestones. The MyFitnessPal App helps me monitor my steps, calorie intake and usage, enabling me to scan QR codes on food packaging so I can see exactly how the food I'm eating breaks down into nutritional values, which then stops me piling on the pounds.

Meanwhile, as cardiovascular diseases such as Coronary Heart Disease remain the leading cause of death globally, taking millions of lives each year, the NHS urges patients not to ignore any potentially life threatening symptoms of heart attack. Chest pain, shortness of breath, dizziness and sweating all require immediate medical attention. And yes, it could just be indigestion but if not, the lack of oxygen or blood to the heart for longer than is necessary can cause serious damage. So, avoiding or delaying medical attention for even the mildest symptoms can be fatal. Early intervention is key to survival.

You might already wear a watch that is embedded with tiny sensors or processors that collect vital information on motion, brain, heart and muscle activity, which syncs seamlessly to a health app on your smartphone or tablet. The data can then be easily shared remotely with healthcare professionals if you are worried about any changes in activity, and even when you are not – meaning you will either get help or reassurance quicker than ever. If in doubt, always call 999. Smart watches may track symptoms and get us into hospital faster, but only a medical professional can treat them. That said, used in combination with health care teams and with further research and development, I truly believe that wearable digital devices are the future of a more joined-up, efficient and life-preserving healthcare system.

For those of us fortunate enough to be able to afford it, annual health screenings are also a godsend. I prefer to spend money in advance on health checks than pay insurance companies for years waiting for them to fix me after something's gone wrong. Every year my check-up gives me the peace of mind of knowing that nothing is wrong, rather than burying my head in the sand and hoping.

Love

SIX FEET OF SEPARATION

There is no fine line between technology and love for me. Whether it's because I am a naturally tribal creature or I am a bit of an all or nothing person, I relish sociability and dread loneliness so I like to be connected 24/7 in life, love and work because it makes me better all round. So rather than causing myself and my loved ones unnecessary stress by battling to keep my family relationships and technology apart, I've worked out that it's better for my wellbeing and the wellbeing of those around me to 'integrate' the two.

In 2020, when social distancing suddenly placed us two metres apart from our friends and loved ones outside of our own household, blurring the boundaries between workplaces and personal spaces, strictly limiting our freedom to find, give, and receive love, it was little wonder that people all over the world embraced video-conferencing apps to combat loneliness and despair, and to re-create feelings of comfort and connection. During lockdown, our mental survival and our only way of maintaining an active and meaningful connection with work, school, leisure and loved ones, rested entirely on a reliable Internet connection.

MAKING A CONNECTION

Finding a way to mitigate the effects of loneliness on our mental health is just as important today as we build our resilience to weather the storms of tomorrow. With technology embedded into our lives now more than ever, we possess the power to reach out and connect with friends and family and both receive and offer support and love anytime, anyplace, anywhere, even if we can't physically be with them for any reason.

Just like me, you've probably experienced loneliness to some degree at some stage of your life. But while being lonely is something most of us only experience now and again, researchers have estimated that chronic loneliness can shorten a person's life by 15 years, equivalent to the impact of being obese or smoking 15 cigarettes per day.[11] Loneliness amongst British men, who have been taught to be tough and stay buttoned up, is a silent epidemic.

No matter how lonely you feel right now, know that you are not alone. With one third of men in the UK – married men included – regularly experiencing feelings of loneliness and one in five admitting to not having a single friend,[12] it's time to address the true cost of loneliness, which is one of the real and present reasons why a man is more likely to commit suicide than a woman. With this in mind I am urging you to make the wisest investment of your life and go in search of true connection in a digital world, and you can embrace technology at any time of day or night to start the process; whether that means reactivating your Facebook account and reaching out to old friends or joining an online support group or forum to forge new friendships.

Men's support groups are on the rise all over the UK and the world, on a shared mission to stop men suffering in silence. There are local groups such as Man Chat Aberdeen,[13] founded by stand-up comedian Wray Thomson, to national groups such as CALM (the Campaign Against Living Miserably) or the global ManKind Project (MKP) with a presence in 21 countries because 'when men of integrity and compassion join together to wake up, grow up and show up, the ripples created change the world'.[14] Joining Menspeak, an online community network that promotes conscious connection in men and healthy masculinity, was described as 'press-ups for the mind and circuit training for the soul'[15] by one member.

But like the gym, it's important to find the right group for you, make it a part of your life and exercise those muscles regularly if you want it to do you any good at all. So the next time you wake up at four in the morning, alone or otherwise, with spiralling thoughts and a sinking feeling in the pit of your stomach, please know that there are huge and immediate benefits to not keeping it to yourself and reaching out there and then.

Work

MINDSET OVER MATTER

For a number of years, I've been a great believer in emerging technology and the potential for new technology to allow many of us to work in dramatically different and better ways and enable a huge proportion of people to do everything their job requires without ever having to set foot in the office. Sadly, it took a global pandemic to prove it.

I've never really understood this herd mentality of office workers cramming onto crowded trains in a bid to be at their desk at 9am, only to read the same emails that they could be reading at home or on holiday while saving themselves time in their day. Before Covid-19, according to the old-fashioned laws of 'presenteeism', if you were not seen at your desk from 9 to 5 then you were probably not working hard enough, or worse, skiving, so working from home has always been considered a perk rather than a right. It's quite possible that the working from home movement would've had to wait another 20 years without the extraordinary conditions and reliance on trust that has been created by Covid-19.

I appreciate that it wasn't possible for all companies to shift over to hybrid solutions or home working, and our key workers had no choice but to remain on the frontline keeping essential services running while saving lives, fighting fires, delivering our food, and collecting our bins. However, since tech-based companies like Twitter and Facebook, who were uniquely positioned for remote working, took the lead, everything has changed. Twitter committed to supporting a distributed workforce capable of working from anywhere, happily ever after, and Facebook immediately pivoted to an indefinite work from home model, anticipating that half its workforce would be completely remote within the decade. The work from home revolution turned out to be so successful that Apple had a rebellion on its hands by 2022 when it announced a return to the office, with happier and more productive staff demanding their right to continue remote working.

Recent unrest within the unions in the UK has also been less impactful than in previous years. All the unions' efforts to max-imise inconvenience while minimising pay losses to its mem-bers by calling two-day strikes with a non-strike day in between (when all the trains are in the wrong places to run a proper service), have largely backfired on them. Covid lockdowns have had a major part to play in this. Large numbers of people have either never returned to the office full-time, or are equipped to work competently from home, thanks to enhanced technology and apps such as Teams and Zoom. They don't need to get on that train, or indeed go to the airport! We all learned how to work from home and we haven't forgotten!

FLYING BY THE SEAT OF YOUR PANTS

In 2020, Covid-19 grounded planes and brought people back down to earth – fast. From the suited and booted, high-flying executives that we were, to taking meetings in our comfy-pants and, in my case, my British Airways pyja-mas, working from home revolutionised our behaviour. Even the royals were able to make jokes about not wearing any trousers on a TV conference call, giving us all the green light to swerve the suits or the smart-casual office-wear minefield.

Working from home was certainly not an easy transi-tion for those who felt very uncomfortable mixing life and work though. I can relate to that. Gradually, over time, it has become my lifestyle of choice, but I used to say that video conferencing could never replace the dynamism and chem-istry and the gut feeling I get from a meeting in person. If I was planning to invest £100 million in a new datacentre or a new acquisition, I'd want the opportunity to look deep into the other person's eyes, to read their body language, to *feel* what they are thinking. So, before the pandemic, my usual course of action would be to go to the office or get on a plane and go and see them. During lockdown however, my BA pyjamas were the closest to frequent flying I could get. And that was ok, because technology still enabled me to have really productive face-to-face meetings, they were just now online and, better still, from the comfort of home. My mindset changed, and I believe so long as we do connect 'face-to-face', albeit virtu-ally, there is still much we can achieve.

In what felt like a lightning flash, the working world's mindset broke free from the nine-to-five shackles into fully remote freedom and seems to have settled into a comfort-able blend. Hybrid working has now emerged as the new working style for most companies and office workers, who appreciate the balance, flexibility and choice of being able to work from the office and from home. If we have adjusted so well to working from home, let's go one step further for our mental health and work-life integration and work from wherever, but more on that later!

Prosper

"No storm can last forever. It will never rain 365 days consecutively. Keep in mind that trouble comes to pass, not to stay. Don't worry! No storm, not even the one in your life, can last forever."

IYANLA VANZANT

FINDING YOUR 45º

Feelings of overwhelm can naturally trigger stress and stress is notoriously bad for your mental and physical health and can lead to early death from heart disease, cancer and other health problems.[16] There's the stress that invariably filters down from major life events like relationship breakdowns, losing your job, loss of friends or family, or global pandemics or there's the minor day to day stress. Both are potentially life threatening and both need careful management. This is why it's vital to use whatever tools you can to decrease stress and increase happiness if you truly want to thrive in life.

Here are some tech-based tools to help you prosper by becoming more focused, organised and calm while boosting your productivity and preventing burnout to help you be at your strongest whenever life threatens to get stormy.

LIVE: BREAK IT DOWN

When you feel like you are on the road to nowhere and not progressing, the key is to monotask, not multitask. Break down your roadblock into smaller bite-size chunks and simplify the job in hand using whatever planning tool makes sense to you. Then, most importantly, focus on one thing at a time. Be realistic with yourself; you'll never complete all your tasks in one go, so rather than worry about them, plan out how you will take action to accomplish them. Think about it this way: each time you complete one task, you're another step closer to completing them all. This could involve the simple act of writing a good old fashioned to-do list, scheduling each task into the calendar for when you are going to do them and ticking them off as you go.

As a simple solution to help you manage the great work-life juggle, take the pressure off your brain with all the mounting tasks you have and truly prosper, you could try an app like Todoist,[17] a very simple yet powerful to-do list app that will help you organise your life and work once and for all. It's designed to help you keep track of important tasks and projects and helps you to break down large tasks into bite-sized ones and then set up due dates and priority levels to help you keep things in order and stop that lingering worry about forgetting important deadlines, bills, meetings and school dates on top of everything else you are trying to juggle. Block time in your diary for personal things such as shopping on Amazon, keeping up to date on Facebook. Whatever it is, put it in the diary and give yourself the STRUCTURED time to do it. This will stop you doing these things INSTEAD of work, which is often the issue when you are overwhelmed and you do anything to avoid addressing the key tasks.

LOVE: OPEN UP

If you don't feel ready to talk to a friend or family member or a therapist, then how about opening up to someone whose chair you regularly sit in? After losing a friend to suicide, Tom Chapman founded an international movement, The Lions Barber Collective, to do something about the biggest killer in young men. On a mission to create a safe place for 'haircuts and headspace',[18] Chapman has built upon the unique relationship between barbers and their clients to prevent suicide and save lives. His multi award winning and endorsed mental health support online course, BarberTalk, trains barbers to spot the signs of mental health problems and notice changes in their clients' behaviour, so they can then ask the right questions, listen with empathy and without judgement, offer support and then signpost them to the help they may need. And each time you pay for a Lions Barber haircut you can feel good about making a difference as some of your money gets donated to raising awareness for suicide prevention and training more hair professionals in mental health support. So think about trying out your nearest Lions Barber[19] or simply remember that next time you are having a haircut it could be a great starting point for a safe and intimate conversation around depression and anxiety, plus you don't have to look them in the eye and, as a regular and frequent event, this is an opportunity to build a rapport and a friendship that stays in the chair. I've had the same hairdresser for over 20 years and the rapport and friendship works both ways. When she was debating whether to start her own boutique, she confided in me and sought my advice as someone that would not judge and would be impartial to her situation. She forged ahead with her venture and has been very successful, by the way!

WORK: BE EVER-READY

When you are dealing with stresses at work, there is often a direct impact on your health, with longer hours at your desk, snatched food that's often not nutritious, late nights out drinking to keep up with the work social circuit and make your presence known, and as a result, looking after your own wellbeing goes out of the window. To counteract these destructive forces, exercise, vitamin supplements, diarising techniques and therapy could be great stress management strategies, but one of the biggest issues that has an immediate impact on our ability to function is a lack of sleep. The good news is that there are several smart solutions out there to help you manage the mental and emotional symptoms of stress and anxiety, such as insomnia, which in itself can exacerbate anger, and frustration.

Your smartwatch or phone can help you track your sleep and let you know when you need more. There are also apps that can help combat stress and calm the nervous system, like the Apollo Neuro[20] wearable, which provides scientifically proven touch therapy in a band for your ankle, wrist, or as a clip attached to your clothing. Soothing vibrations interrupt stress triggers, the 'fight or flight' response – that makes you feel like you're in danger even when you are not – change our energy levels and rebalance body and mind. A wearable hug for the nervous system that tells the brain that you are safe and in control, Apollo Neuro is proven to lead to an improvement in HRV, the most reliable biometric of stress, which reduces the risk of injury, insomnia, chronic pain, cardiovascular illness, anxiety-related disorders and depression. Using the accompanying smartphone app, you can choose from one of six modes depending on whether you want to perform, relax or recover. Choose the 'Energy and Wake Up' mode to help you get out of bed in the morning, without the help of caffeine. Select the 'Clear and Focused' mode to fight off stress and stay clear and calm to meet a challenging deadline. Build the 'Sleep and Renew' mode into your bedtime routine to help you fall asleep quickly.

Other tech solutions to help you manage insomnia and stress include Oura[21] rings to monitor your sleep and other biometrics, sense changes in your body associated with stress and give you feedback. Or Muse[22] offers a digital sleeping pill that provides biofeedback and helps you fall back asleep if you wake up in the middle of the night.

CHAPTER 2

COMMUNICATIONS

*"Dignity of human nature requires that we
must face the storms of life."*

MAHATMA GANDHI

C ommunication has been alive for as long as we have, but the mechanisms of how we pass words, ideas, information, love and understanding from A to B have evolved through the centuries. From cave paintings to TV, and smoke signals to text messages, we've moved on from the most basic of physical and verbal signals, to the messages and even emoticons we see embedded in technology we use today. Whether we are passing through life under clear skies or in storms, nowadays our ability to communicate can significantly affect our stress levels, especially if we don't have a reliable Internet connection.

This chapter is about how you can optimise your physical and emotional resources and communicate more clearly, effectively and confidently with family, colleagues and friends, whenever and wherever you want or need to, 24/7, come rain or shine.

Live

WORDS WINNING WARS

No matter what our chosen channel of communication, what we say and how we say it can make or break a situation; it can make someone feel really good or really bad.

And good communication can make a huge difference to our lives, particularly in times of crisis. Language is most certainly power, in all forms of communication. Take Winston Churchill's powerful speeches, rich with emotive language, metaphor and powerful imagery, which galvanised a nation during the dark, stormy days of World War II. Churchill's memorable soundbites during the summer of 1940 such as 'We will fight them on the beaches' played a vital role in motivating people and ultimately helping to win the war. His mighty roar strengthened Britain's resolve, mental resilience and boosted the flagging spirits of soldiers on the frontline, inspiring them to pick up their weapons to fight on after their allies had fallen. This was a far cry from Russian President Vladimir Putin's attempt to justify his invasion of the Ukraine to his state-controlled nation as a 'special military opera-tion'[23] and an act of self-defence.

It just goes to show how language can be a tool of mass communication or a weapon of mass destruction – and it must be used with care. These days, social media plays a huge part in our communication, from influencing decisions to educating the masses. Unfortunately, it can also cause great physical and emotional pain in the wrong hands.

CARELESS TALK COSTS LIVES

In April 2020, with Covid-19 at the forefront of our commu-nications, Donald Trump, then President of the United States, horrified medical experts the world over when he made flippant and vague comments about using disinfectant as a cure for Covid-19. He quickly passed these off as 'sarcasm' and was immediately denounced by medical experts. Most people would have laughed at such a stupid idea, but the impact of his words soon had a ripple effect, and emergency poisons hotlines across the US received a terrifying spike of enquiries concerning the effects of ingesting bleach and other cleaning products – proving just how potentially lethal a few words can be.

A year later, 'Trumpism'[24] struck a deadly blow. Trump supporters, refusing to accept his defeat in the 2020 US elec-tion, stormed the Capitol government building in Washing-ton on the 6th January 2021, battling police and forcing law-makers into hiding. Social media companies came under fire for how they had failed to police the far right extremists, online influencers and even Trump himself from fanning the flames of disinformation in the four years leading up to the event. By the time Facebook and Twitter finally took action and banned Trump from their platforms in response to the event, it was already too late. Four people were dead. Careless talk really does cost lives.

Mass communication was vital to the Covid-19 vaccine rollout. However, introducing a novel vaccine so quickly into the general public to stop the spread of a virus is no easy task, and this was not helped by a flood of false information across social media channels. Myths like the vaccine delivery being a secret way for Microsoft to implant microchips into people, altering DNA or causing sterility generated a potentially fatal swell of vaccine hesitancy. In fact, this kind of misinformation behaves a bit like a virus itself. False news stories tend to spread faster, deeper and wider than true stories, cascading from 'host to host' across Twitter hashtags, WhatsApp groups and your great-aunt Mabel's Facebook profile (yes, she opened one). And to make matters worse, a fake story is unshakeably persistent. In fact, in 2019 the World Health Organisation listed vaccine hesitancy among the top 10 threats to global health stating that it 'threatens to reverse progress made in tackling vaccine-preventable diseases.'[25]

So the message here is clear: be careful with your words, and don't be swept up in a sea of fear with everything you read or hear online or in the media. Propaganda is alive and well, but our individual contribution to communication can literally change somebody's life. If unsure, test your theory on reputable sources before sharing or reacting. We can't always control what others say and do, but we can control what we say and do in response.

Love

LOVE IN A COLD CLIMATE

We all have different ways of coping with adverse situations, and of course that often impacts the way we communicate. Some of us like to talk through our problems, and some of us prefer to sit in quiet contemplation. I'm an extrovert, so I find that talking helps me to overcome life's challenges. Stewing in silence is not for me. As I'm talking, especially if I'm talking with someone with whom I'm able to make a 'connection', I'm invariably able to draw from their energy and that is so powerful.

When I was in the South Pole, effective communication and team talks were essential to survival. You also have to keep moving to stay warm, and to stay alive. One day during our polar expedition we were chased by a weather front; you could actually see the storm clouds rolling in behind us. The storm was as high as a skyscraper! We had to pick up the pace and work together as a team, digging deep to communicate, motivate and inspire each other – all very hard to do when your moustache is frozen to your nose and your mouth is numb with cold! I kept reminding myself that every torturous step was taking me out of danger and bringing me one step closer to being back in touch with my loved ones. It's *all* about perspective. You change your perspective, and your feelings change, your actions change, the results (of your actions) change, and your world changes.

'IT'S NOT THE MOUNTAIN WE CONQUER, BUT OURSELVES'

I really relate to famous explorer Sir Edmund Hillary's words because I'm naturally drawn towards challenges greater than myself. Whether it's agreeing to run a full marathon a day for 40 consecutive days or trek 120 kms in -60° temperatures across the Antarctic plateau to raise money for vital research and treatment of brain tumours, I don't like to sit still for long. Pushing myself to the limit and putting myself out of communication with the people I love the most helps me grow and find perspective. It's uncomfortable but it also makes me appreciate things more when I get back home. It's these extraordinary experiences in my life that have made me realise the untapped potential and inner strength that lies within all of us, but sometimes we just need a bit of help to know where to find it and what to do with it when we do find it.

COMMUNICATING WITH LOVE

The deep, unspoken connection between trust and communication starts the moment we enter this world, and trust and transparency form the bedrock of all good relationships. I admit that they're something I've had to come to learn, accept, and practice over time, thanks to the good relationships I've built with Shalina, my family and friends. But I can't begin to tell you the number of times my trust has been betrayed, and when it starts with your own father, you can choose to sink, or swim. I chose to swim, and fast.

As my brother Billy wrote in a letter to me soon after our father died: *'We become who we are, from our very beginning. No matter what each day brings or how bad life appears at dusk, the dawn brings new opportunities... happenstance gives us a second chance to steer destiny back on track.'*

My father was a violent bully, a wife beater and a criminal. Not a man to be trusted. As a child, my mother and I spent a long time on the run from him, but he continually overcame our attempts to escape him, even when we moved countries. During my last encounter with him, he grabbed me by the collar and held me in front of oncoming traffic, threatening to leave me in front of the next truck if my mother didn't come out of the hotel where we had been hiding in Zimbabwe, near the border of Mozambique. He was subsequently arrested and deported (again). Thankfully, instead of following in his footsteps, my siblings and I went in the opposite direction. And by eventually succeeding in our lives, we insured ourselves against any risk of history repeating itself.

I'm not saying that second chances guarantee happy endings. There are emotional scars that no amount of love, communication and good fortune can erase. When you've lived through hell, you have to work hard not to end up back there again. There's always going to be signs of wear and tear. But you have to take responsibility for that. You have to ensure that history isn't repeating itself in the way you manage your relationships. At times I've noticed traits in my personality that remind me of my father; for example, in the way I used to communicate with my son and my wife, Shalina. Traits that could seriously damage our relationship if I let them. The most important thing is to recognise your own actions and reactions and get in control of how you want to use your communication power in your language of love. It's an ongoing journey...

Work

SHOE ON THE OTHER FOOT

Years ago, I negotiated a data centre purchase from my good friend, Eduardo Azar, a true Argentinian gent. There was a lot at stake and clear and urgent communication was vital for me to keep control of the process by keeping the sale away from the open market and strictly between the two of us. If I had any chance of sealing the deal on the Friday before the weekend got under way, I needed to act fast. So I thought carefully about how and when to communicate for best effect.

Firstly, I knew he was a practising Jew, so our time would be up by sunset when he would start Shabbat, the Jewish Sabbath, which, being mid-winter, would be earlier than normal. Secondly, I knew that he happened to be up in Scotland playing golf, and the days are even shorter up there in winter. So I phoned him around midday on the Friday and said 'it's going to be an earlier sunset where you are compared to where I am, so what's my drop-dead time to get you the final proposal?' He said, 'Michael, get it to me by 2.30 absolute latest.' So I moved heaven and earth to complete all the paperwork just in time for the deadline and deliver an amazing deal: He got paid 90 times more than his initial investment and we made six times our money on it! And like many people I've come to do business with, Eduardo and I went on to become good friends. He later explained that he chose my offer above all others because he trusted the way I did business. He liked the fact I had gone to great lengths to communicate with him and work around his needs. And for that reason he was confident that this level of trust would translate into business, that I would look after his management team and follow through on my promise to retain them. He told me my thoughtfulness about the timings of sunset meant he signed the documents immediately after I phoned and put them in escrow until the final paperwork came through! Communicating about what your colleague, partner or client needs, not just you, will always get you a better result.

OPEN DOOR POLICY

I've learnt other lessons in effective communication that are still as relevant now as they were back then. For example, what's going on outside work inevitably has an impact on what happens in work. Listening to and supporting colleagues when they're going through a tough time has a beneficial impact on their mental health and their longer-term productivity. It's during the difficult times that we all need someone to talk to, to bounce frustrations off, whether that's work colleagues, or family, or both. For me, there is no clear division between work and home – it's all my life and part of who I am as an individual.

During my Telecity days, I would take senior colleagues out for dinner as often as I could, not as an opportunity to talk shop but to properly check in with them and find out how their relationships were going, how their kids were getting on at school, or any personal worries they might have that I could help them with. They truly valued the time and attention I gave to them during those sessions. They felt listened to without judgement, able to pour out their worries and know that anything they shared would stay within those four walls. As their boss, it also gave me a chance to figure out how I could get maximum effort and engagement without pushing them too far. It was good for all of us to talk, air any grievances and keep our personal and professional lives moving forwards. Is there someone you could talk to at work to give them a better understanding of who you are and how you are feeling now? Or is there someone you could open your door to and listen to? Opening the lines of communication with colleagues can resolve issues for you and them if you give it a chance.

Prosper

FINDING YOUR 45º

*"Communication is power. Those who have mastered
its effective use can change their own experience of the
world and the world's experience of them."*

TONY ROBBINS

For someone whose trust has taken quite a beating over
time, being able to communicate confidently in life, love and
work in order to prosper in all areas is truly liberating: it
feeds my soul, fuels my emotional wellbeing and nurtures
lifelong friendships, but I also appreciate that it's one of the
hardest things to do. Technology gives me the tools I need to
say and do the right things, but it doesn't control my actions
or my emotional self-regulation – that's down to me. If you
find it difficult to speak up and make yourself clear, here are
some tips and tools to help you overcome any social anxiety,
become a better communicator and build trust so you can
truly prosper and thrive in all scenarios:

LIVE: BREAK IT DOWN

More often than not our ability to communicate well starts with how we feel about ourselves and what we tell ourselves, especially in a world where comparison with others is rife, and we subconsciously want to know how we are stacking up compared to everyone else.

The only person we should try to be better than today is the person we were yesterday. It's about recognising that every day we are the result of every past decision we have made up to that point. And tomorrow we will be the direct result of the decisions we are making today. So if we are doing things today that will make us better tomorrow, and we continue that pattern day after day, we are always going to be in the process of becoming our best. One way to do this is to ask yourself the following: Where will the choices I am making today lead me? Am I doing better today than I was yesterday? Do I have goals in place to help me do things better tomorrow?

The knowledge and ability we possess to live the next day better than the previous one is something to be celebrated. Life is fragile, precious and uncertain so this incredible freedom, privilege and choice we have to choose our words and actions wisely and lead a better life each day will ultimately lead to a more fulfilled, fun-filled, and rewarding life.

LOVE: OPEN UP

What's your love language? The 5 Love Languages[26] can be a real game changer when relationships get a bit lost in translation. Based upon Dr. Gary Chapman's long-time work as a marriage counsellor, it's a simple but powerful premise that we all give and receive love in 5 different ways or 'love languages'. These are: 'Words of Affirmation', 'Acts of Service', 'Receiving Gifts', 'Quality Time', and 'Physical Touch'.

Controversially, most of us have one or two dominant love languages and these are often different to the ones preferred by our partner. How we show, how we are shown, and how we receive love are not necessarily the same thing and can have a great impact on how we communicate love to another person, and whether or not they can actually recognise that type of communication as love. If you express your love through *your* preferred love language, it may go unnoticed by your partner, because it's not *their* preferred language. For example, if your love language is 'Gifts' but your partner's love language is 'Acts of Service', you might think they don't appreciate your gifts because they don't have much impact. Or you might think you need to spend a lot of money or time on gifts, when in fact you don't! Instead of wasting money on unappreciated gifts, you could try spending time helping with household chores or helping them out in some way and see the difference it makes. Suddenly you are talking in a language both of you understand, and that connection makes for a new type of communication that heals wounds, breaks down barriers and ensures you are both feeling loved.

Once we start to analyse and understand each other's love language, it's much easier to identify where the disconnect is coming from and instantly improve it by showing love in the way the other party understands. There's an app, podcasts and a free love languages test on the website[27] to get started. These also apply to non-romantic relationships, so can help with communicating with children and teens too. Life is complicated enough so taking the time to understand the language your loved ones talk can lead to a stress-free and simple route to relationship success.

WORK: BE EVER-READY

Communication is critical to the success of any organisation. It's the spinal cord connecting all the different limbs of a business. It's the join up between leaders and front-line managers, suppliers and distributors, employees and customers, which is positive when it's all going well, but under stress can mean that problems in communication quickly spread to other areas and create conflict in the workplace.

Employers consider good communication skills more important than qualifications or technical ability, because confusing or unclear directions can waste hours of productivity. Like the mastery of any skill, put some practice into your communications at work and navigate your way more clearly, directly and effectively to an improved life both at work and at home. There are tools to help if you struggle with social skills, suffer from communication anxiety or even if English is your second language and it's creating a barrier to creating connections. GetMeeAi[28] is an AI-powered coaching app for individuals and teams to measure and enhance their communication, social, and emotional skills by using an algorithm that securely observes how you communicate and then tailors the coaching according to your needs. Self-development is never a wasted opportunity, so take some time to analyse your own communication skills and progress your performance to really improve your connections.

CHAPTER 3

BUSINESS

*"I can't change the direction of the wind, but I can
adjust my sails to always reach my destination."*

JIMMY DEAN

I've both sailed and struggled through life on a riptide of extraordinary events and experiences, from 'fair winds and following seas' that have made things plain sailing, to high waves and strong swells that have threatened to scupper me completely. No matter what the conditions though, I've learnt not to put my belief in 'strategy' or 'five-year plans' because no matter what it's like when you set off, you can't predict the future, and you certainly can't control the weather or the wind. Instead, listening to and learning from other people's advice and experiences have helped me make my way.

This chapter shares some of my stories of overcoming challenges and hardship in business to inspire you to develop a resilient growth mindset that enables you to seize opportunities for success in a world of ever-changing business conditions.

Live

GROUNDLESS GROUND

Groundless ground is like having an invisible floor in front of you. Even though you can't see it, you have to have faith that it's there. I describe it as knowing you need to cross a chasm and being told to just put one foot in front of the other. You have no *grounds* to believe the *ground* is there, yet still you must take the step. It actually feels more like taking a huge leap of faith than a small step towards success, and although that leap may test your fears and vulnerabilities, it could also become the first step towards seismic change.

FIGHT AND FLIGHT

I experienced the feeling of groundless ground from a very young age. While my violent father was away in Australia, my mother and I managed to escape to Rhodesia, but far from being safe, we ended up in the middle of the Civil War. Life there was difficult. Most days it was a toss-up between whether we would be petrol-bombed or shot at by terrorists while travelling in convoys between cities. And then our greatest fears were realised when my father found us, and in fury he tried to strangle my mother. We survived this terrible episode and managed to get help, and eventually my father was deported but we still were not safe. Despite breaking the law again, he kept coming back, going to dishonest and manipulative lengths to do so – such as bribing emigration officers or even hiring a helicopter to find us from the background of a photo of me sent to him. We lived in a tense, uncomfortable and gut-twisting reality, fearing for our lives every single day. We had taken a leap of faith that day we escaped, and on the surface that faith was not rewarded because it wasn't instantly obvious. But as life then continued, shifts in our lives and our mindsets became real and have had an impact ever since.

LIFE BEGINS WHERE FEAR ENDS

Looking back, I had some tough decisions to make at a very young age, and I could have fallen prey to my fear, and let it control my choices, or I could use it to learn how to turn fear to my advantage and convert it to fearlessness. Let's face it, there's not much you can learn from a parent figure who flips from absence to violence – apart from the determination not to end up like him! I didn't have a role model to teach me these important life lessons, so through my own mental and sometimes physical leaps of faith, I figured it out for myself. One particular experience is a great example of how fear can control you, or how you can control it.

While living in Africa, I had grown very used to the harmless monitor lizards who would shuffle across the floor of the house. So, when I was at a friend's house one day and we saw a tail poking out from behind the pedal bin we all just assumed it was a lizard. Then my friend's mother asked me to get the lizard out and close the kitchen door. As I got to the bin, the tail spun around and before I knew it, a spitting cobra reared up level with my face and looked me straight in the eye. It was petrifying. If just one stream of deadly venom from the cobra hit my eyes I would be blinded, and subsequently dead!

I was terrified but transfixed; stuck in fear. It was like my brain had temporarily disconnected from my body and I couldn't move my feet. Suddenly, I became aware of some movement in the corner of my eye as my friend's mum firmly and calmly swept into the room, picked up a broom, smashed the cobra with the head of the broom, picked it up by the tail and threw it out the door. Job done. 'You could have done that,' she tutted scornfully to me, and got on with making lunch.

It felt brutal but she was right. In that split second I learnt never to wait and see what happened next, or to be paralysed by fear. I learnt to be the master of my own destiny... or at least try to be!

From that day onwards, I took responsibility for my own actions – positive or otherwise. Stay or go, move or don't, every decision I make is mine, and every consequence or result is mine too. Believe me, there have been times when I've felt out of control and ready to let life lead me down the wrong path, but then I remember that no matter how big or small my move – whether it's deciding to roller skate down a dual carriageway at the age of 16 because I didn't have the bus fare to get to work, or deciding to jump on a plane at the last minute to attend a board meeting the next day in Hong Kong, the buck stops here. This sense of responsibility could feel like a burden, but it's actually one of the most liberating and empowering approaches to take to finally feel in control of your own destiny.

Love

ROOTS AND WINGS

I wouldn't wish the childhood I had on anybody, but it certainly gave me the courage to turn my fears on their head. And although I can't bottle that feeling and share it, I can use it to help you confront your fears and become empowered by your fearlessness. Past conflicts, old fears and unnecessary worries can have a habit of chipping away at our resilience, but it doesn't have to be this way, for you or for your colleagues in business.

Goethe once said about parenting, 'There are two things children should get from their parents: roots and wings'.[29] Whether you are already in top management making decisions that will impact others' lives, or aspiring to climb the ladder, it's so important to remember that the best kind of business leader is like the best kind of parent, one who provides support, roots and wings for their business, colleagues and employees to help them prosper and thrive through the good times and when the going gets tough.

Like good parents, effective leaders sometimes have to make unpopular or risky decisions and sometimes they make mistakes. But ultimately, they are prepared to and indeed know when to step up, step back, or go to the ends of the earth. Just like my mother did when she seized her make or break moment to take us across the world away from danger, only to unknowingly risk further danger on the other side. Now I'm not a gambler when it comes to people's lives and livelihoods, but I know when to trust my gut, and I know that if I always act with love, I will ultimately give my colleagues both roots and wings.

I applied some pretty radical management techniques during my time as CEO at Telecity, which still raise eyebrows around the boardroom table today. When I wanted to encourage my team to break old patterns of thinking, I treated them to an unprotected swim with sharks. When I needed to diffuse tension between colleagues who had previously been bitter rivals, I took them up to the Arctic Circle where they had to sleep two-to-a-bed for body warmth. I then wrote these stories down so they could travel through time and help the business leaders of today think differently; to break the mediocre and traditional way of doing things. Maverick? Yes. Irresponsible? Absolutely not. All of these decisions were made with a firm knowledge that it was my responsibility as a business leader to energise, enlighten and empower my team; the more maverick the better!

THE TOUGH GET GOING

When I started at Redbus Interhouse in 2002 as sales and marketing director, it was on the brink of going bust. The company was burning cash at the rate of millions of pounds a month and no matter how fast I worked to bring the contracts rolling in, we only had weeks left to do something that would help us survive. We needed a miracle! Cliff Stanford, the founder and CEO, had also just bitten off more than the company could chew by forking out on a brand-new data centre in Prague that we could not afford to run. Within days of the grand opening of our new site, the great rains and floods that afflicted Prague in 2002 swamped the building. It felt like a disaster but turned out to be the perfect storm we so desperately needed to survive.

In the middle of the chaos and confusion, I followed my gut and took a leap of faith. The site was insured for £40 million but anything near that would be impossible to get before the company slipped into administration. I went to the insurance company and cut a deal that would get us enough cash to survive – and fast – saying, 'It's worth £40 million, but give me £8 million today and I'll go away.' It was risky but things were so bad by this point there was nothing to lose. It was this way or no way, and the outcome would only be worse if I failed to take any action at all. I took a big risk because I cared so much about the company. Thankfully, it paid off and Redbus survived a period of extreme turbulence until the next round of investment came through.

Work

RULES OF ENGAGEMENT

Twenty years on, the turbulence of Covid-19 turned office life as we knew it completely on its head, proving my long-held belief that there is no one-size-fits-all approach to business, and that applies no less to company culture.

In the wake of the pandemic came the dawn of new eras including 'The Great Resignation', 'The Big Quit' and 'The Great Reshuffle'.[30] But for many it was 'The Great Rethink'. After enduring the emotional trauma and upheaval caused by the pandemic, record numbers of people have been quitting their jobs and rethinking their priorities and what they want from their work culture: more flexibility, more of a say in where, when and how they work, and most importantly the support and empathy of their employer. The novelty of perks like ping-pong tables, unlimited snacks or even a bigger paycheck have worn off, employees simply want to feel looked after and listened to.

A recent McKinsey study has revealed that workers who feel a sense of greater purpose tend to perform better, are much more committed, and are about half as likely to look for a new job.[31] It's worth taking the time to figure out your definition of meaningful work. Is it contributing to a higher cause? Putting skills to use? Feeling part of a team? Or, is it what earning a wage allows you to do outside work that really makes a difference to you? The companies that take the time to find out and respond meaningfully will come out on top, and you can evaluate what is making you feel happy, or making you feel hollow, by assessing where your work fits into your purpose.

The future of the workplace is bright, hybrid and flexible, where work is an outcome, not a time, place or transaction. Trust and human-centricity will drive employee productivity, business performance and ultimately sustainability in the new normal. Personal work styles and preferences are as varied as the people that make up a total workforce. Now more than ever, as companies watch attrition levels rise to painful levels, they must focus on playing to the strengths of their people, give employees the autonomy to figure out the hybrid work configuration that works best for them and focus on making work really work for the people. With the majority of companies agreeing in principle to a hybrid working model going forward but remaining a bit sketchy on the finer details, you might naturally be feeling a bit anxious about what the future holds, and you certainly won't be alone in that.

This is a good opportunity to take the lead considering what it would take to either make you happy at work, or for you to make your colleagues happier, and see how you can communicate this for the best outcomes. If nothing changes, then don't fear moving on either, it might feel like you are staring at groundless ground by starting a new role or even starting your own business, but trust your gut and don't accept 'unhappy' as standard.

FIRE FIGHTING

Flexibility, or rather the lack of it, is often the cause of great stress. That's why I've always let my employees do their essential personal tasks within their work hours if they need to; when else are they meant to do it if they work long hours all week? Granting them the trust, freedom and flexibility to manage their own time, whether in the office or from home, or both, reaps incredible loyalty payback and stops people feeling like they are just constantly fire fighting. I'm sure you feel the same about your time. Great freedom brings with it greater responsibility, and your teams will recognise that. You will foster loyalty. A good example of when this loyalty came to fruition for me was in 2013, during my days at Telecity, but this time the fire fighting was real.

There was a huge fire in the building next door to our Paris operation, a serious blaze that destroyed the other building and threatened to leap across to our data centre. Having evacuated salespeople and customers, when the firefighters came into the building and insisted that my MD Stephane and his handful of remaining core staff were to evacuate immediately, they refused because they wanted to remain operational and in service to customers. Even when the head of the fire brigade explained that if they didn't leave now the exits would be blocked by their engines and that they could be stuck there indefinitely, they were resolute.

I would never have asked them to do that. No leader ever writes in an employee handbook that people should have so much loyalty to their company they should stay put in the event of a fire! They made the decision to stay for themselves and by themselves because they wanted to, because they were 100% committed and connected to their purpose and a flexible business vision that breeds steadfast loyalty. After a very tense 18 hours where the flames were virtually touching the building, they felt able to leave. This was an amazing display of fierce loyalty in what was a truly life-threatening situation.

Prosper

FINDING YOUR 45º

*"A tree with strong roots can withstand
the most violent storm."*

DALAI LAMA

Businesses operate in an ever-changing world, one in which we are constantly having to predict, react, and adapt to technological and tectonic shifts that impact directly on the way we live and work. Living in a 'permacrisis' may feel as terrifying and fear-inducing as swimming with sharks and sleeping in ice hotels, but in the middle of the storm often lies the best opportunities for us to adjust the sails to the winds of change and head off in a brave, new direction.

LIVE: BREAK IT DOWN

My good friend, Harvard MBA and business yogi, Jagdish Parikh, who I used to bring in to run hypnosis sessions at Telecity to de-stress the team, has a good take on fear. He says, 'If you are really ill, what are you going to do about it? If there's medicine to take, take medicine. If there is no medicine to take and you're going to die, well you are going to die. Either way, don't worry about it'.

His point is that you have to learn not to worry, because worrying about something that hasn't happened is like paying interest on a debt you haven't even drawn down on. Fear of what might happen saps your energy and your ability to focus on what you need to be doing now. Try reading about how other people have converted fear into fearlessness and figure out what might work for you. Nelson Mandela spent 18 years breaking stones with a 2kg hammer as a prisoner on Robben Island before he became President of South Africa. No great leader has ever got to where they are without having to overcome fear and failure. Take Edison's 10,000 attempts to create a light bulb or Dyson's 5,126 attempts to invent a bagless vacuum cleaner;[32] they had to fail fast and keep going, but they got there in the end.

LOVE: OPEN UP

When you're feeling under pressure trying to stay afloat under the weight of busy work diaries, looming deadlines and managing personal relationships, life can feel overwhelming and impossible. It's easy to get swept up into an emotional storm of complex and extreme feelings – whether that's anger, anxiety or stress, rocking around like a boat caught in the middle of a storm at sea. In these moments, we feel like we can't get control, and even when we do, we can't completely eliminate those negative feelings from our minds and our bodies. But there are a few really effective in-the-moment techniques to switch your brain back from chaos to calm. When you're feeling really anxious or even on the edge of a panic attack, it's important to find the best way of steadying yourself until the storm passes, for example:

Square breathing: Imagine four points on a square, and see each one in your mind's eye. As you mentally focus on the first point, breathe in for four seconds, at the next point hold for four seconds, at the next point breathe out for four seconds, and at the last point hold for four seconds. Repeat for a few minutes until you've restored some calm in your body and can focus on your next actions.

Connect with your senses: Distraction therapy can support you to feel calm quickly and in any situation. Name five things you can see, four things you can touch, three things you can hear, two things you can smell and one thing you can taste. Repeat for a few minutes until you feel calmer. These are also great techniques for helping to restore calm in someone else; for example, a stressed partner or child.

WORK: BE EVER-READY

With hybrid teams increasingly dispersed between home and office, there are fewer opportunities for spontaneous office interactions like last-minute team lunches, informal hallway 'hey, nice job' or 'how are you doing?' bonding, or a quick strategy session by the coffee machine. These small informal moments of social connection can be a game changer and are well known to improve workplace wellbeing, boost productivity and reduce burnout. Steve Jobs famously designed the location of the toilets at his Apple headquarters to ensure cross pollination of employees and ideas. So the chances are that if you're hybrid working, working remotely, or operating from an office that feels a bit emptier than it used to, then you might well be missing those sparks of camaraderie, connection and community that fire up your creativity and innovation.

If your workplace setup is creating feelings of isolation in you or your team, think about how you can restore some connection both physically with coffee meetups, and Zoom meetings, and get some chat going virtually to help people feel less alone. Re-open those channels of communication by using a tool like the Donut[33] app with your colleagues. You can sign up through Slack[34] – another very useful collaboration tool – and opt-in to recreate those casual serendipitous water-cooler moments and get randomly connected with new teammates, lively coffee break debates and peer learning.

CHAPTER 4

FINANCE

"In order to realise the worth of the anchor we need to feel the stress of the storm."

CORRIE TEN BOOM

I n today's fast-moving, ever-changing economic conditions, trying to make too many financial predictions is probably about as useful as putting a finger in the wind. As the world floats perilously through one financial crisis after another, let me help you confidently drop an anchor in all the chaos and confusion.

This chapter is about how to build your own financial resilience and confidence by discovering a higher value to life, love and work and a deeper level of prosperity and fortune that has absolutely nothing to do with pound or dollar signs.

Live

SURVIVAL OF THE FITTEST

Our survival over thousands of years has depended on real people, real resources, and real achievements. We can survive without money, but we would perish without food and water, which ultimately today depends upon money. Early humans relied on a system of swapping goods and services if they needed something they were not able to source from their immediate, natural surroundings, or if their capabilities didn't allow them to achieve it. This was known as 'bartering'. Before coins, units of exchange have ranged from cows to cowry shells, feathers to stone wheels, teeth and salt, to rum and parmesan! Goldsmiths in the 1600s were effectively the first bankers in the UK. They would give early traders receipts for gold coins that were deposited with them and then would convert the receipt back into gold when they returned. These receipts became early bank notes as people realised that it was much easier to carry around pieces of paper than precious metals. Today, we exchange our goods and services using money that we don't even see. I wonder what early man would make of the cashless, contactless online marketplace we live in today.

A PROBLEM SHARED

It's very normal to experience money troubles at some point in life and they can be overwhelming enough to test even the deepest reserves of resilience. But if it's got to a point that your financial worries are starting to take over your life, it's so important to talk to someone about how you're feeling. Money links to feelings of responsibility, perceptions of success and self-worth. It affects how you choose to work, rest and play, which can make financial stress even more difficult to cope with. Money affects so many aspects of life, love and work that worries about money invade both waking moments and sleeping moments, making everything seem hard to cope with.

No matter what you are going through, if your money is running out, and you are concerned about your job or your business, please don't keep it to yourself. If you can find the courage to speak up, your friends and family will love and respect you even more. Money can cause temporary happiness or unhappiness, but the value of love and friendship goes far beyond being anything that you can buy. A problem shared really can be a problem halved, and speaking up can help you get through the worst of times.

MONEY'S TOO TIGHT TO MENTION

I was twelve when we returned to England from Africa. I'd been shot at so many times and even hit once in the leg, enough was enough. My mother was reluctant to return to the UK, but we just couldn't take it anymore. There's resilience and then there's just plain foolishness, so the decision was made to leave. But it wasn't plain sailing by any stretch of the imagination. At the airport in Africa they took everything from us: our outer clothes, our luggage, our money, our jewellery, everything. They even took the letter we had with us, with valuable stamps stuck on it which we carried for this very eventuality. Nothing of value got on the plane! Apart from our passports and our boarding cards all we owned were the clothes on our backs; we had been literally stripped down to refugee status. This was even before the time of mobile phones! But this was no time to feel sorry for ourselves.

When we got to the UK we had nowhere to go so we moved into a squat in Stockwell in central London with my stepfather and got to work. That's where we broke into the music business, or rather, we broke into old, condemned houses waiting for demolition. Very often we'd find old pianos that people couldn't be bothered to move. Rubies in the dust. We'd rescue them, tune them up, roll them down the Old Kent Road and sell them in East Street market for £20 each. By creating our own little enterprise, we did what we had to do to put food on the table and stay alive.

Love

ALL YOU NEED IS LOVE

Love and work don't typically go too well together. But bringing your love and appreciation to work can result in a surprisingly positive return on investment in your business. Showing gratitude to your colleagues and business contacts doesn't need to cost money, it often just needs some different thinking, and it can bring outstanding results.

Good business depends on good relationships. And all the core values of love – truth, trust and commitment – apply just as much to business relationships as they do to personal ones. For example, in 1998, I was sorting out ICL's mainframe maintenance company in Copenhagen. As the fifth manager in only three years, I had to go above and beyond to win the battered hearts and the confidence of my team to save the business from financial collapse. Rather than lazily throwing money at the plan, I invested time, energy and goodwill into a pretty hair-brained and risky relationship-building exercise, which set off a remarkable sequence of happenstance that I could not have planned better myself!

MAGIC CIRCLES

It was December 1998, and with Christmas just around the corner, I bought a map of Denmark, plotted the home addresses of each of my employees who had children and rented a Father Christmas outfit. I then spent the weekend driving around Denmark, delivering gifts to each house. The news spread like wildfire about ICL's nutty new Santa-impersonating CEO.

It just so happened that on the Friday night before my magic mission, I'd been trying on the Santa outfit in the office before taking it home for the weekend. One of the sales managers popped his head in and asked what on earth I was doing. I explained, and he said while I was at it could I possibly visit the recovery ward for alcoholics at the local hospital that his wife worked in. I went with him that very evening. It was a very moving experience. The patients were overwhelmed with emotion, grateful that anyone would bother to come and visit them at Christmas time. Some of them, the medical staff told me, were unlikely to make it through Christmas.

Afterwards I ordered a taxi to take me home. My costume prompted a lengthy conversation with the taxi driver. We talked about all sorts including my day job as a CEO of a technology company, why I happened to be moonlighting as Santa and the time I spent learning magic tricks with Magic Circle,[35] the world's premier magic society. It turned out we had a lot in common. In addition to his work as a taxi driver, he was also a ventriloquist and a clown, and had spent much of his life travelling the world bringing joy and support to impoverished children in developing countries, returning to Denmark every nine months or so only to earn enough money driving taxis to continue his mission.

I gave him my card and a few months later he phoned me up, 'Hi, it's Jon Christensen, the clown taxi driver. They're opening a new children's ward in the state hospital in Copenhagen. I'm doing a show: do you want to come along?' I piled up a bunch of laptops, games and other goodies donated by Microsoft, Fujitsu and Siemens onto a trolley and made my entrance in a puff of smoke.

LEAD FROM THE HEART

Back at the office the next day it turned out that the opening of the ward and my visit to the hospital had hit the headlines. 'Apparently CEO's do have a heart,' said the papers. As a result, The Danish Department of Health also got in touch to say they were running a tender for an outsourcing role and wanted us to bid for it, because anyone who demonstrates that level of care and attention for kids was likely to do a good job for them. We entered the pitch and won the deal.

This ripple effect of goodwill just goes to show that good things happen when you invest your time and allow the value of love to rise to the surface, rather than just seeing people as a commodity or thinking 'What can I get out of them? How do I make the most of this person?' Not only was it quantified on a company balance sheet, but I managed to win hearts and create a longer-term buffer zone of trust and happiness to help protect against any future difficulties, disagreements and conflict.

In business, and in life, we need to accept that we are the owners of our ability to be happy. And the more we can lead from the heart and spread happiness to others, particularly in the darkest periods, the happier it makes us feel too. It's a win-win.

Work

THE VALUE OF TIME

On the subject of happiness, until you value your time more than you value your money, you will never be truly wealthy. Not according to Benjamin Franklin, a leading figure in early American history, whose legendary phrase 'time is money' from his book, 'Advice to a Young Tradesman'[36] has lived on for years. In this context he meant that time should be spent wisely so that one can earn money, and if this time is wasted, then opportunities to make money are lost. This remains true today. However, when you're young with more life ahead of you than behind, time just seems irrelevant and money feels like the be all and end all. It can be too easy to value the external results of time: money, possessions and fame, rather than the less visible results, like relationships, health and mental wellbeing.

There's nothing like a global pandemic to make you re-evaluate your time on this planet and how you want to spend it. Once you start to value time as a currency, like money, then you can really start to assess how you can spend your time most effectively to get the best out of it. You can either turn to technology tools and systems to help track and manage your time or simply start to notice, value and model your internal habits and attitudes that produce the best over-all results.

The world is accelerating into a remote, hybrid and post-pandemic future of work, where employees value cultural benefits, purpose-driven roles and flexible hours. Now is the moment to assign more time and a higher value to investing in your people for the most holistic return on that investment.

PLANTING A SEED

Investing in people with your time is a bit like investing with money – it's all about planting seeds for both parties' future prosperity. Just like plants, some of your investments of time will bloom immediately, some won't grow roots at all, some will spring up and then die off, and some will grow slowly and then suddenly flourish. Some will require lots of attention to grow to the next phase, some will be more self-sufficient, but the more seeds you plant by investing time in others, the more returns you will ultimately reap.

Life can be very uncertain, and even when you've invested your time you may not know what's going to come out of the ground or what the flower is going to look like when it blooms, but that doesn't really matter as long as you keep planting those seeds. Even in difficult times, when you are feeling tired or lacking in energy, if you continue investing in your people, the time will come when you can sit back and enjoy watching your team blossom and grow without you.

Prosper

FINDING YOUR 45º

"Prosperity seems to be scarcely safe, unless it be mixed with a bit of adversity."

HASEA BALLOU

The word 'prosperity' comes from the Latin 'prosperus', meaning 'favourable' in the sense of good fortune. In time, it has evolved to have the additional sense of being affluent, of having a fortune, being prosperous in terms of monetary gain.[37] This chapter has been about exploring that original idea of prosperity in terms of a flourishing, a flowering, a realising of potential, rather than just acquiring money. Here are some ideas of how to build financial confidence, mental resilience and awaken a new feeling of 'prosperity' that will genuinely enrich your life, love and work even when the storms are raging.

LIVE: BREAK IT DOWN

Financial stress covers a broad spectrum of emotions. There's no one way of feeling it and we all have different responses depending on our own situation at the time. But no matter what the problem, and no matter how hard it may feel to find, there is always a solution. In times of trouble, I've found it helpful to flip my mindset and think about what I have now, not what I don't. Focusing on what makes us fortunate, be it creativity, strength, fitness, knowledge, experience, can help to reset the mind. Here are a few lines I try to remember to keep things in perspective:

1. There is no point using a limited lifetime to chase unlimited money.

2. There is no point earning so much money you cannot live to spend it.

3. Money is not yours until you spend it.

4. When you are young, try not to use too much of your health to chase wealth; or when you are old, you'll have to use your wealth to buy back your health.

5. Happiness is not having what you want, it's wanting what you have.

6. There is no point working so hard to provide for the people you have no time to spend with.

LOVE: OPEN UP

Money can be a tough topic to talk about at any given time. What we earn can feel like a number that represents our value and identity. To be clear, it absolutely doesn't. Your value is made up of so many things other than money.

You might be struggling to support yourself or your dependents or having to choose between heating and eating, or know someone who is.

When we're experiencing financial stress, this can cause great anxiety, panic, and a feeling that there's no way out. Feelings of shame, fear, frustration, anger and hopelessness, as well as pressure and judgement (often from yourself) can have a very real impact on your health and mental wellbeing.

No matter what your issues are or how they began, there is always practical or emotional support available. The Campaign Against Living Miserably (CALM) have advisors[38] ready to talk right now. You can also get help even by opening up to people already in your life, like your GP or, on a practical level, your accountant or financial advisor.[39] It's amazing how many people we have around us who might just have the answer if we could only dare to share how we are feeling. Please don't suffer in silence any longer. You are not alone, day or night. Relevant charities and support lines are included in the back of this book.

WORK: BE EVER-READY

If you are starting to have worries over the security of your financial future, there are trained experts and specially designed technology to help you get in control before things start to get out of hand. Even starting with a simple spreadsheet with all the details of your household budget can give you the facts and become your financial GPS. Financial planning apps, like Emma,[40] can help to keep your finances under control by weeding out the wasteful subscriptions you keep meaning to cancel but are still paying for, and revealing spending changes you might not have noticed. If you value your time just as much as money but are feeling that you never have enough of it, revolutionary apps like Rescue-Time[41] will help you become more effective and productive by measuring and tracking what you do on computers and mobile devices then giving you intelligent insight into how you spend your time.

Martin Lewis's Money Saving Expert[42] website is a great place to start with a wealth of useful money saving guides, tips, tools and signposts. Meanwhile, the charity Step Change[43] offers free debt advice and an online debt tool to help you face and overcome debt problems and get life back on track.

A friend of mine who at the time was living in New York, once came to me asking for advice in a pretty desperate state. A former successful banker, he had decided to go-it-alone and start his own consultancy business. He had a young family, a large downtown apartment and all the weight of the world on his shoulders. He was closing in on a major deal, but his finances were running out fast and he was about to miss his rent payment. This was causing him untold stress, despite the fact that he was almost about to close on his deal. 'What if I can't pay the rent?' he said. 'What will my wife think of me?'

He had a three-year-old daughter and was feeling overwhelmed. I asked him if we took away the rent as an issue would he be able to get to the deal and change his world, and he said yes. I asked him how long he had been a tenant in that apartment. He said nearly 10 years. '…and in all that time have you ever missed a payment?' I asked. 'Never,' he replied. So I said 'Go to your landlord and explain the situation. He trusts you… after 120 on-time payments he will feel comfortable giving you a few weeks' grace if you ask him for it, especially IN ADVANCE of it falling due.'

He did just that and got the grace period he needed to get his deal done.

By breaking the problem down into bite-size pieces and dealing with the specifics, it was no longer an insurmountable issue. And it was never as bad as he feared it could be!!

CHAPTER 5

EDUCATION

"I am not afraid of the storms for
I am learning to sail my ship."

LOUISA MAY ALCOTT

We must never stop finding opportunities to learn and grow, particularly in times of crisis, and Covid-19 certainly presented us with a steep learning curve that required fast navigation. The pandemic suspended our education system as we know it and the unthinkable happened: in the UK, high school exams were cancelled or changed significantly for two years running and schools the world over had to close their doors to most of their students to protect everyone's health. For every parent and teacher faced with the challenge of remote schooling at very short notice, technology offered digital solutions, apps and resources to keep education going, in one way or another.

In the heart of the storm, thanks to technology, learning remained very much open for business. We even had a jam-packed schedule of virtual lessons held by celebrities, which included everything from Joe Wicks (P.E.) to Dr Chipps (science, engineering and computing).[44] Some might say education even improved in some way…

In a world where knowledge is a mouse-click away, traditional education is no longer the 'only' way. This chapter will inspire you on a new journey of educational enlightenment. By reimagining education not as something that finished after school or university years, but as a lifelong model of learning that brings out the best of you. By harnessing the best that technology has to offer, you'll discover untapped reserves of talent and be ready to seize continuous opportunities for self-development and learning.

Live

DIGITAL NATIVES

Back in 2015, I delivered a keynote speech in Barcelona on how technology has influenced education. I used an example of how the average 14-year-old in Western Europe is able to absorb up to four hours of content for every hour they are actively engaging with content, due to technology platforms. Meaning they can come home, put Netflix on, open up their MacBook, WhatsApp a friend, post a video on YouTube or TikTok, and stream their favourite music through Spotify. All at the same time. It's as natural as brushing their teeth for these digital natives, who have grown up with technology.

I had clearly struck a nerve as a woman suddenly jumped up in the audience and blurted out, 'Are you actually condoning the fact that teenagers today spend all their time on devices?' I stopped the talk, we were not even at the Q&A part yet, but I had to explore my immediate hunch, 'Señora. I presume – given the anger in your voice – that you have a teenager at home who "suffers" from this phenomenon?' She replied, 'Yes, my daughter!' I paused for a moment and thought of a better way of making my point. I said, 'Imagine that your daughter comes home from school, fires up her iPad to start doing her homework online, switches on the TV to watch a Natural History Channel feature about the Phoenicians, texts her school friend in Maths Club with the solution to a particularly tricky calculus question, and pops her headphones on to listen to Rosetta Stone teaching her Mandarin. You would be inviting all your neighbours round to witness your star child!' She nodded in agreement and sat back down. It's too easy to blame technology for our choices, but I doubt she would have been so critical of technology during the Covid-19 lockdowns. Technology isn't bad, it's how it's used that defines the outcome.

The pandemic forced global education systems to take brave steps into this century, embrace technology and foster a more flexible attitude to work that transcends classroom walls. In the wake of the storm, we can all make choices that help us and discover the silver linings that technology quite clearly offers. If you haven't already, take the time to learn from your children and seize the opportunity for digital enlightenment. Whatever your experience of school and higher education, the past is past. The ground underneath is shifting quickly but the good news is that we're shifting with it.

HEAD DOWN, HANDS ON

My own education didn't start easily. Running away to Rhodesia, finding myself in the middle of a civil war and becoming homeless created its own educational challenges. When I left school at 16 I picked up an apprenticeship with Rockwell Automation as an Electronics Engineer. It was the making of the man I am today. My commute to Rockwell involved a fourteen-mile daily round trip on rollerskates – it was the most economical mode of transport for a poor 16-year-old with a lot of energy and enthusiasm but no money for a bus ticket!

At Rockwell, I learnt some accounting, spent time with the sales team, gained experience in panel beating, production and Quality Assurance, and then suddenly I was invaluable to the company because I understood each and every element of the business and how it fitted into the bigger picture. And as well as working every hour under the sun to get the best out of my apprenticeship, I also worked part time at the local food market, setting up the fruit and veg stall. Before I knew it I had a heap of transferable skills and experience that I could take forward into any career. But it didn't come easy and there was no magic formula. It was simply about hard graft and the drive to succeed.

By the age of 21 – when most people would still be racking up debt at university – I was Managing Director of Goupil. In later years, I secured my appointment as CEO of Redbus PLC, listed on the London Stock Exchange, and eventually masterminded the hugely successful merger with Telecity. The rest, as they say, is history. But the point is, my personal success in business and leadership was not dependent on a degree or qualifications. There were a couple of lucky breaks along the way, but my entrepreneurial ethic to always work hard and strive for success enabled me to shoot for the stars, right from my grass-roots beginnings. I truly believe that we can all be who we want to be and that it's true grit, determination and focus that can give us as much, if not more, power to succeed than any formal qualification.

Love

OUT WITH THE OLD

It's very natural to feel a bit daunted about what the future holds when it comes to our children and the myriad of decisions that revolve around their education. Afterall, how do you plan for what you can't predict in a world of constant change? But whether they have a plan or not, there's no doubt that technology will set them up for success in a competitive global economy and a rapidly evolving world of work, and this change has started in the classroom.

For the last two hundred years, teaching has followed a one-size-fits-all approach with neat, straight lines to suit our linear brain patterns. From reception to Year 13, UK classrooms have been run by teachers who deliver lessons that start and end with a bell. A suffocating combination of excessive workloads, box ticking and paper pushing has been squeezing the joy out of the system for the teachers. Even before the pandemic, a fifth of UK teachers hoped to be out of the classroom within two years, while two fifths of educational professionals reported that they wanted to quit in the next five years because they felt the education was no longer all about the kids.[45] But now, for a system that's broadly followed the same shape and rhythm for generations, technology could dramatically shift the goal posts. If you look at class sizes in UK state schools today, for example, you can't blame teachers for wanting to quit. One teacher versus thirty kids in the class? Truly terrifying. And at the other extreme, a ratio of 1:3 is financially unsustainable, but what if artificial intelligence could act as those ten extra teachers?

EMBRACE CHANGE

Looking at the future of teaching, could machines take charge of the things that a teacher managing the behaviour of 30 children might understandably miss? Embedding AI within educational resources could enable teachers to differentiate pupils' learning and drive each child on their own learning journeys. Robots could take the heat out of the teacher's excessive workloads – marking work, data entry and reporting – freeing them up to connect with their true purpose and meaning again. A few years ago, we didn't think pupils could be taught online, but now we know that anything is possible.

That said, technology will never substitute a really great teacher. Our teacher role models have been trained to provide moral guidance and cultivate fundamental human capabilities: empathy, curiosity, creativity, imagination, emotional and social intelligence and leadership in a way that a robot cannot. However, I'm a great believer in technology doing jobs that either people can't do or helping them to do the job better. If technology has the potential to help a great teacher become even greater, it could be the fast track to ultimate job satisfaction for many in educational roles.

Work

EAT, SLEEP, RE-SKILL, REPEAT

Emerging technology means that the shelf life of our skillsets is getting shorter and shorter. If we want to keep up with the changes, firstly, we need to recognise gaps in our skillset and then take the necessary action to fill those gaps. By proactively steering your own ongoing skills development to stay ahead of the curve, you'll improve your marketability for years to come.

Instead of worrying about being relevant today, use this time to upskill and enable yourself to grow. To become your own problem solver, ask yourself the following questions:

1. Are my skills still in demand?

2. If they are, how long are they likely to be in demand for?

3. What skills could I learn today that will set me up for success in the coming years in case my current skills are no longer in demand?

If you carry out this skills assessment every few years, you'll stay ahead of the game and combine your experience with the latest skills. Work on the premise that the half-life of a learned skill is five years (which means that every five years, a skill you learned five years ago is about half as valuable as it was then) and make sure you update your skills every few years to get ahead of that curve. Remember also that experience is a skill in itself. Being the best at what you do can also give your skills longevity...

SELF-DRIVE YOUR SHELF LIFE

An example of a role that's under imminent threat is commercial driving. Truck drivers, taxi drivers, bus and train operators and agricultural workers could see that their future jobs are under threat by the fast-approaching dawn of self-driving and autonomous vehicles. Rather than waiting for self-driving vehicles to come on the scene (which may seem like many years away but look how quickly the pandemic accelerated change in other industries), they must start building new skills before their current roles are put at risk. The new driverless era could provide a wealth of exciting opportunities for upskilling as well as re-skilling. As we come to regard driverless cars as a service rather than a product, new roles will spring up as part of a wider 'smart' infrastructure that requires human oversight, maintenance and development. This will create a more digitally focused job pool with opportunities in fleet management, maintenance, software development and the widespread construction of smart infrastructure.

With the rapid rise of AI tools such as CHAT GPT, many roles that could not be replaced by robots are now also coming under threat. Lawyers, analysts, doctors, the list is endless of careers that could be delivered faster, cheaper and better than by humans.

If you are thinking about a job change or a skills refresher, the most future proof careers consist of work that *complements* machine work, or work that largely depends on human skills and therefore cannot be replaced by a computer. No matter what your job is now, think about how you can work with technology to improve your prospects for the future.

Ultimately, AI will not replace humans, but humans that use AI will replace humans that dont.

LEARN TO BE AGILE

If you're not quite ready to jump ship, then you could learn to be more agile. When the pandemic hit, companies like Delta Air Lines, General Motors, and Unilever went into agile mode in response to the crisis. This enabled them to launch their pandemic response in record time. With sanitation suddenly a much higher priority for airline customers, Delta created an entire division dedicated to cleanliness. General Motors repurposed its factory lines and built thousands of ventilators within a few months, and Unilever adapted one of its deodorant manufacturing lines in the UK to produce much-needed supplies of hand sanitiser for the NHS. Agile management can be applied to any project in any industry and is about giving teams the freedom to self-manage and self-organise, to test ideas and iterate solutions rapidly without having to always go up the chain of command for approval.

If you can learn and then teach others to operate with agility at all times, you'll keep your business fit and able to keep pace with the rate of change and especially in times of crisis.

The key to success is embracing a process of continuous improvement rather than always aiming for the finished article. The sooner you can accept that it's about the journey not the destination, the sooner you can start to really enjoy the journey.

Prosper

FINDING YOUR 45º

"Life isn't about waiting for the storm to pass. It's about learning how to dance in the rain."

VIVIAN GREENE

Over the past few years, we've all had our minds opened to new experiences and continuous learning opportunities. As the pandemic has reminded us, we grow and learn best when we are forced out of our comfort zones, and we can use these times of challenge to build our skill sets, put our trust in technology and ride the waves of change as we build our own new normal.

You will never know everything you're truly capable of until life forces you to prove it to yourself. Recognise that in your quest to become the best version of yourself, you have to put the effort into improving the talents you already have, while continuously searching for an undiscovered well of abilities and talents that are yet to rise to the surface. Many of them will surface during times of challenge and pain. Others will surface as you gain more wisdom. Remind yourself that your daily goal isn't to be better than anyone else but to seize every opportunity to learn and improve yourself.

LIVE: BREAK IT DOWN

You possess limitless seeds of talent and ability. Some that are yet to be planted, some that are budding, and some that are already blooming. Take some time to get to know yourself a bit better. Write a list of your own real talents and abilities. Then ask yourself, how can I further develop them to be the very best they can be? Which of my natural abilities have I not yet begun to grow and develop? You can even use this time of self-development to make a list of the habits you would like to change and set goals to help you transform these for a healthier future – in love, life and work. Write everything down and give yourself realistic deadlines to hold yourself accountable to making it happen.

LOVE: OPEN UP

If you're feeling a bit out of your comfort zone while trying to keep up with the rate of change of technology, tap into the younger generations around you: your own kids, nieces, nephews, extended family and friends. Remember, these guys have grown up in a gaming, 3-D, socially connected environment and will be able to answer all your questions and help you grow your skills and opportunities when it comes to technology. Rather than just making assumptions based upon your own experience of education, spend some time connecting with them and understanding how they learn best in a digital world. In turn you can share the most valuable skills in your leadership toolkit and play games to teach them strategy, negotiation and the art of presenting and public speaking. You really don't have to look too far from home to broker a meaningful skills exchange and build deeper relationships under your own roof. I am always asking my kids how to do certain things within apps, or on my phone.

WORK: BE EVER-READY

You could also teach yourself to harness the power of your 'reality distortion field' (RDF) through visualisation. RDF was a term coined by Apple's Vice President of Technology, Bud Tribble,[46] to describe the rare charisma of the late Steve Jobs, Apple's co-founder.[47] His incredible level of self-belief meant he refused to accept limitations that stood in the way of his ideas and was able to convince himself, and others around him, that they were capable of achieving the impossible; that no difficulty was insurmountable.

Your reality distortion field is the reality you project to the world about yourself based upon what you believe about yourself. It gives you the ability to choose your reality, so why not choose the reality you want most?

Try out the EnVision[48] app for free and start on your journey to self-empowerment, belief and confidence. Practising visualisation techniques for just ten minutes a day will start to create the motivation and momentum to shift that mindset, unlock your creative right brain, access your RDF and activate the law of attraction, to draw in the people, resources, and circumstances you will need to accelerate your performance, health and success goals and inspire others to achieve theirs.

CHAPTER 6

MENTAL HEALTH & WELLBEING

*"When the storm rips you to pieces, you get to decide
how to put yourself back together again."*

BRYANT H. MCGILL

will never forget the end of an 18-month leadership development programme that I participated in, when Jagdish
Parikh, a Harvard MBA and business yogi, walked in and
said, 'Forget everything you have just learnt, the whole lot,
just forget it. It's all worthless unless you are worth something to yourself.' He was right. Self-worth is everything, but
all too often the rush and pressures of life make it easy to
sideline our own self-appreciation. Yes, we make sure to

brush our teeth and wash our clothes every day, but our emotional wellbeing is right at the bottom of the to-do list.

This chapter is about how you can start to build a stronger foundation of self-worth, and a healthier approach to your personal needs will support you to live your life to the fullest.

Live

A HEALTHY BLEND

I've spent years thinking about what the perfect work/life combination looks like. I'm not alone in this. And of course, it looks different to different people. But essentially it's about having a personally fulfilling job that pays enough money not to be miserable but also enables me to enjoy family life. For me, the two coexist, but so many people continue to regard business and family as separate entities, with work often coming way above other life events in importance. For example, when it comes to family events, many people don't think twice about cancelling them at the last minute because of work, or just turning up late, and yet they wouldn't dream of being late for a business appointment. Actions like this do often feel necessary, but they push past our personal boundaries and take their toll on our relationships in the long run.

It's easy to forget that both family members and business colleagues require a healthy dose of our attention in order to flourish. Rather than keeping them apart, we need to ask ourselves, how can one complement the other? How can business leaders who automatically tend towards nourishing their businesses also make the same contribution to a flourishing family? My advice always has been and continues to be this – don't struggle hard trying to balance the two. Integrate your work and personal life together, and you'll be much more successful. After all, you are the same person!

REFRAMING HAPPINESS

Do you find yourself extremely focused on creating success at work and define your happiness in these terms? It's easy to become hooked on the perception that happiness is driven by success, thinking things like: if I can get a promotion, I will be happy. If I can grow my company, I will be happy. The thing is, the more successful you become, the higher the bar for your definition of success rises, making it even harder to truly *succeed* in life. If your happiness hinges on this concept, you will end up never really being 'happy', because at the very moment you achieve your expectations, your goal posts shift, and the definition of what makes you happy moves out of reach once again.

I've been my own victim of success in the past but have also realised that success is also relative to the situation, and many times that way of thinking has saved me. When I was CEO of TelecityGroup, the stock market took a dive one day and the company's share price fell sharply. We weren't alone: everybody's share price plummeted that particular day. But the market had crashed and my spirits followed suit.

At my lowest point, investors and analysts were calling me and saying they wouldn't be selling that day, whatever the share price was at the close of business. I suddenly realised that if we could finish the day within, say, 3% off where we had started it would in fact have been a relatively good day ('relatively' being the key word). As soon as I let go of my perception of a perfect outcome and accepted a relatively good one, my whole nervous system suddenly calmed down. It's interesting that today a daily 3% movement in share prices is commonplace and happens almost every day. Talk about relativity!

Since those early years, it's helped me to reframe my perception of happiness and success as an attitude floating in relativity. The attitude of accepting pain and disappointment as part of pleasure. An attitude to move away from self-obsession while being resolutely focused on my core values and commitments. An attitude of embracing good fortune without being possessive, along with accepting bad fortune without being disappointed. The attitude to 'let go' when it no longer serves me to hold on. This attitude has helped me to thrive even in an environment full of uncertainty and challenge, much like the one we live in today. Could a shift in thinking help you too?

Love

CLOAK OF SHAME

When it comes to reframing your reality, there are many great examples in the world. One of my favourites being the fabulous artists, The Connor Brothers (who aren't actually brothers!). This duo introduced themselves to the urban art scene in 2012 under the pseudonyms Franklyn and Brendan Connor.

Eventually revealing themselves as two British art dealers, Mike Snelle and James Golding, the two 'brothers' had been born into a secretive cult known as The Family in California, and both men had suffered with resulting mental health issues: Snelle with suicidal feelings and depression, and Golding with addiction. They explained that they invented the identity of The Connor Brothers as 'a cloak to cover the "shame" that both felt about their lives, and to protect themselves from the discomfort of public exposure.'[49]

It all started in 2012 when James decided to pick up the phone to his friend Mike one evening to ask if he was ok. Mike was going through a particularly severe bout of depression and James just happened to catch him during a frightening and desperate moment in which he confessed his suicidal feelings. After an emergency referral to a psychiatrist, Mike was diagnosed as having bipolar disorder and started his journey to recovery with therapy and medication.

As a way of overcoming their personal battles, the men moved in together and started to produce art works together as a form of therapy; although the prospect of releasing the works scared them. In their attempt to stay low-profile and out of the spotlight, they concocted an elaborate backstory of how they ran away from the cult at the age of sixteen and ended up in New York where they turned to art to interpret the real world.

The art market became as obsessed with their identity as the work they created, which is quirky sketches, overlaid with captions referencing popular culture, history and politics. They managed to keep the ruse up for a couple years, but as their works became more and more popular, sought after by world-leading art houses Bonhams and Christies, they knew that they risked their professional credibility if they didn't come clean about their identities.

JUST ONE ACT OF KINDNESS

Now ambassadors for mental health and suicide prevention charity CALM (The Campaign Against Living Miserably),[50] James and Mike are passionate about using their art to raise money to support the cause, awareness around male suicide and to explore the links between masculinity, mental wellbeing and creativity. The pair joining forces was never about achieving success or fame, that was all just a very fortunate by-product. Their art is their form of therapy, which they are now using to make a powerful difference to other people's lives.

The Connor Brothers are living proof that focusing on something that is a skill, strength or a release can be therapy in itself and can even help others so I would fully encourage you to discover the right form of 'therapy' for you. Whether that's learning a new skill, brushing up on a hobby or going to talk to a therapist, please embrace any opportunity to divert, absorb or manage persistent feelings of stress and anxiety.

In the UK, suicide remains the biggest killer of men under forty-five. So I am also sharing this story as a reminder of how just one small act of kindness from a friend or colleague – like James picking up the phone to Mike that evening – can be both life-changing and lifesaving. I have a number of Connor Brothers artworks at home. One of my favourites is entitled: *'every saint has a past, and every sinner has a future…'*

Work

THE SUM OF OUR PARTS

I cannot speak highly enough of the merits of implementing mindfulness to achieve a happier, healthier and less stressful workplace. Every year at TelecityGroup I brought in Jagdish Parikh, the very same yogi that taught me so much many years before, to work with my leadership team on just that. One of the things he taught them was how to 'hypnotise' themselves; to calm and control spiralling thoughts and emotions.

According to Jagdish we are the sum of our parts: body, spirit, soul, brain and experience. This combination defines who we are and is not a single physical thing. Just like we own and manage all elements of our business, we are responsible for each of these parts of our own being. If we can train ourselves to 'get out of our bodies' and act from a third-party perspective, then we are in a far better position to effectively manage our thoughts and emotions. You know when you find yourself arguing over something really petty, but you can't help yourself and things get more heated than they need to be? Or you insist upon telling others what is the right thing to do while being unable to follow your own advice? Step back and look at the argument, more often than not you will realise how unnecessary it is. I do this a lot. When I find myself getting up on my soapbox, I trigger a signal to myself that reminds me to go into third-person mode. It's easier to see the logic when you are disconnected from the situation.

SEE THE LIGHT

Jagdish used a traffic light analogy to help us identify our emotional triggers and develop self-help strategies. A simple analogy is to imagine you're driving to a meeting and you are late. You hit a red light and it feels like it lasts longer than usual before turning green. That red light winds you up because you could feel that each second it was red, you were getting later and later, and more and more angry and panicked. It's too easy to just blame the red lights, but that will get you nowhere, just step back and learn next time to set out 15 minutes earlier.

If you do get into a 'red traffic light' moment, flip your mindset and decide that the red light is going to be a trigger for calm; instead of winding you up it could actually become your signal to de-stress. By really believing it, you will feel it. And next time you feel tensions brewing, tune in to people's body language. You will see physical signs of frustration, irritation or embarrassment: twitching knees, drumming fingers, clenching jaws. These are their 'red lights'. Help them work out what their trigger is. Rather than getting wound up by the 'red light', embrace it as the early warning system; once you or they can recognise it, use it to override a negative reaction.

By practising this technique I can usually work out when my patience is about to pop. At that point I reboot and think to myself, 'What am I trying to do here?' I might distract myself to diffuse my irritation, pick up a coffee pot, move my phone on the table, feel my feet on the floor. A fleeting two or three second window to refocus my attention and reset my mind prevents me from flying off the handle. What else could you apply this thinking to in your life?

Prosper

FINDING YOUR 45º

"No one's life is a smooth sail; we all come into stormy weather. But it's this adversity – and more specifically our resilience – that makes us strong and successful."

TONY ROBBINS

The constant drip-feed of social media, emails and news alerts delivering endless information on climate change, globalisation, financial crises and political complexity are enough to make your heart race and your self-worth plummet on a regular basis. Even in the eye of the storm you can be the owner of your happiness and project that happiness on to others.

The first step is to define what makes you happy, because feeling happy is as much physiological as emotional. When you are happy, endorphins are released into your body, which in turn make you far more receptive to outside inputs, more alert and more active, and so the more endorphins whizzing around your body and your brain, the more chance you have of achieving success in life, love and work. So when we think success will bring us happiness, it's actually the other way round... happiness brings success!! Try taking some small steps to boost your happiness hormones, your self-belief and your overall wellbeing in the midst of great uncertainty.

LIVE: BREAK IT DOWN

Some of us seem hardwired to look on the bright side, while others get absorbed by the negative stuff. More than five decades of research suggests that an optimistic outlook helps you stay healthier, sleep better and live longer.[51] You can start to train yourself to be more optimistic and boost your self-esteem and sense of mastery by:

Positively reframing: Whenever you catch yourself expecting a catastrophe, stop. That's only one possibility. Instead, try thinking about a negative or challenging situation in a more positive way. This could involve thinking about a benefit or upside to a negative situation that you had not considered or identifying a lesson to be learned from a difficult situation.

One shot of optimism before bedtime: You are most likely to hold on to the thoughts you think and things you tell yourself just before falling asleep. So try to make them positive. Keep a notebook by your bed and just before you turn out the light, write down the three most enjoyable things or things you are grateful for that happened during the day, and make a note of something you are looking forward to doing tomorrow. Focusing your brain on gratitude and positive thoughts will reduce stress and anxiety and prevent you from getting stuck in that negative thought loop that stops you from sleeping.

Imagine your best self: Set aside 20 minutes and find a quiet area. Select a time in the future, maybe six months or ten years from now. Imagine yourself in that future where things are going really well, e.g. your dream start-up is turning a healthy profit or you've landed that huge client you have always wanted. Then spend the next few minutes mentally exploring it. How would you feel? Where would you be? Who would you be with?

Next, spend 10 minutes writing a description to answer questions about that future self or how it feels to have achieved your biggest goals. Don't worry about getting it 'right' or stopping too much to think or getting hung up on grammar and spelling – just write whatever comes to mind.

This exercise will immediately improve your mood and your outlook so try building it in as a weekly ritual and replaying within different scenarios across your life, love and work.

LOVE: OPEN UP

Like the story of The Connor Brothers, sometimes just one act of kindness can change someone's life and will enrich your feelings of self-worth in so many ways. Helping others can promote changes in the brain that are linked with happiness by triggering a release of oxytocin (the love hormone), which fends off cortisol (the dreaded stress hormone). Interestingly, the higher your levels of oxytocin, the more addicted you get to helping others because when oxytocin is boosted, so are serotonin (the happy chemical) and dopamine (the pleasure hormone).

You could start by safely checking in with a vulnerable neighbour, signing up for the GoodSam app[52] or checking out ways to get involved in your local area such as helping to organise a fundraising event.

Consider volunteering your time and business skills to your local food bank[53] or as a mentor to help young people get started with self-employment.[54] Have a good clear-out and donate clothes or old household items to families in need, transfer credit card points to charity[55] or give blood. At work, be a role model and take advantage of charitable workplace perks like paid volunteer days or match funding or encourage your colleagues to do so. If your company doesn't offer them, then be the spearhead for change. Your renewed confidence, optimism and self-belief will radiate out into the world making your community, your work and your home happier, healthier places for everyone. Yes, I know what you're saying: 'I don't have the time'… trust me… you do.

WORK: BE EVER-READY

In his 2009 memoir *What I Talk About When I Talk About Running*, author Haruki Murakami says: 'Most runners run not because they want to live longer, but because they want to live life to the fullest. Exerting yourself to the fullest within your individual limits: that's the essence of running, and a metaphor for life.'[56]

If you are in a difficult place in your life, running could offer you a pathway out of it, as it has for me and so many others. For people with mild to moderate depression, regular exercise may be a more effective alternative to prescribed antidepressant medications or talking therapies. It will help you to live longer, reduce stress and make you happier.

This all sounds good on paper, but when you're feeling low it's easy to keep procrastinating or finding excuses not to do it. If you want to start your running journey then download Couch to 5K[57] on your phone today for free and you will be running 5 km within 9 weeks, even if you've never run before. It works because it gradually builds up your fitness and stamina through a realistic and achievable mix of running and walking. Week 1 involves running for just a minute at a time!

Running with a friend or a group will help you stick to your healthy habits. Grab a friend or colleague or contact the #Run and Talk[58] scheme run by England Athletics and supported by the mental health charity, Mind, to find a running group near you that also offers mental health support.

If you aren't quite ready to pop on those trainers, download Happiness Expert Gretchen Rubin's Happier app from Apple Store or Google Play[59] for a free, three-month trial. A bespoke, practical toolkit to help you build and track habits to become happier, healthier, more productive, and more creative.

CHAPTER 7

CHARITY & PHILANTHROPY

*"One friend in a storm is worth more than
a thousand friends in the sunshine."*

MATSHONA DHLIWAYO

Since the dawn of society, the human race has been defined by the 'haves' and the 'have-nots'. Wealth is not new. Neither is charity. Put them together then you are well on your way to addressing the fundamental problems of mankind: philanthropy. In its earliest form, the word philanthropy, from the Greek 'philanthropia', simply meant 'love of humanity'.[60] Today this can be shown in so many ways.

Taking small, philanthropic actions can set you on a life changing path. It doesn't have to be about donating large sums of money. The truth is that anyone can become a philanthropist without even putting their hand in their pocket. It's more about acting with compassion and wisdom to nurture and support people. This chapter is about inspiring and empowering you to start thinking and acting like a philanthropist.

Live

MONEY TALKS

While national and global disasters have a universal impact, it's always the most vulnerable who suffer most. The pandemic cruelly exposed this harsh truth. Those already challenged by their mental health experienced further deterioration. School closures compromise family's mental resilience and the wellbeing of those already living in poverty for many reasons. And most tragically, the charities that would normally have come to their rescue found themselves staring into a funding abyss, with their helping hands well and truly tied as the sector took hits from all sides.

Charities working at grassroots level depend on regular cash injections from large-scale fundraising events that could no longer take place around the world. When the pandemic hit, charitable causes suffered from a squeeze on personal giving, as households rapidly redirected resources to essentials. Other vital income raised from charity shop trading and renting out rooms to activity groups or meetings disappeared as people stayed indoors. Public sector contracts with other charities, businesses, schools and the government were compromised or cancelled, which sent the sector into a cash flow crisis from which many closed, and many will take years to recover.

Well-run charities model themselves on well-run businesses, both placing resilience and sustainability at the heart of their operations. And in a volatile world, where coronavirus, war and recession pose persistent threats to our security, no business model can rely on things to simply carry on as they were. One option for charities on the brink of collapse is to tap into automation and benefit from the dividend of time, which can be used to reduce staff burnout, build stronger client relationships and address the root causes of the societal problems they exist to solve.

MULTIPLICATION

It was incredible to see the use of smart tech by the charity sector explode during the pandemic. For example, food banks deployed robots to pack meals; homeless support teams used chatbots to give legal and mental health advice; and fundraising departments turned to AI-powered software to identify potential donors. But it doesn't have to stop there. This is a once-in-a-generation opportunity for charities who are pushed beyond belief to reimagine their charitable mission and accelerate social change by stepping carefully and wisely into the adoption of smart tech.

The Trevor Project is an example of a growing wave of 'Smart Non-Profits'.[61] The organisation provides crisis counselling to young lesbian, gay, bisexual, transgender, queer, and questioning (LGBTQ+) people, many of whom are at higher risk of suicide, not because of their sexual orientation or gender identity, but because of how they are mistreated and stigmatised in society. This smart non-profit has taken time to understand and implement a process of 'cobotting', the combination of people and smart tech that brings out the best in both. Riley, their proprietary chatbot, is always on hand to train counsellors and volunteers by providing real-life simulations of conversations with potentially suicidal teens. This not only expands the organisation's scope for training and supervision but enables it to stick resolutely to its human-centred mission of ensuring that teens are always talking directly to another human being. This is one of many inspiring initiatives where technology isn't subtracting from the human experience; it's adding to it, and it's an example to us all of working smarter, not harder.

Love

SHARING SUCCESS

A US not-for-profit, Goodwill Industries was founded on the premise that it should serve the principal of 'not charity, but a chance'[62] for people in need. How does that chance come about? The answer is philanthropy. Being a philanthropist was a natural life choice for me. It was another chance in a long line of chances that helped me to overcome my difficult beginnings. As an adult, I found myself questioning how my success at work could translate into helping others; how could I be part of an all-encompassing, bigger force for change?

Focusing on using what I have to help others over the years has helped me keep my feet firmly on the ground. If I'd given in to the luxury and decadence of the booming tech industry that lay at my fingertips in the great Internet boom; if I'd allowed myself to be swept away by my own self-importance as a leader, I would have failed. Instead, I felt this overwhelming urge to use my own experiences to motivate others to pick themselves up off the floor or simply to show solidarity for those who have never, and might never, get a chance to even try. And for me, it's not enough to just think of giving in terms of money. Whether it's sleeping rough alongside other CEOs in the street in front of the London Stock exchange, running 40 marathons in 40 days or pulling myself and a sled across the Antarctic plateau, I hope that my actions speak louder than any words I could say. As far as I'm concerned, I want to challenge myself and feel the discomfort and pain that will help me connect with my fundraising aims. I have to go big or I may as well go home. I have to feel that I am making a difference; to show that I mean business and I'm willing to suffer too if it will get a bigger result that will in turn help the causes I'm passionate about.

At the end of the day, when I endure a challenge for charity, I remember that I always get to clock off, but the sick, homeless and marginalised cannot. It's not just 24 hours sleeping rough or even 40 days of running in their lives; it's their entire lives. I could never sit back and say 'my work here is done' when there's such unhappiness and need still in the world. And for someone who originated from poverty and violence, it would be hypocritical to do so. I am pretty tough on myself when it comes to explaining the motivations behind my own philanthropy. It's about nurturing a creative and critical mindset to get to the heart of an issue and create fundamental change. It also helps me keep my everyday problems, worries and stress in perspective.

SLEEP OUT TO HELP OUT

I count myself as one of the lucky ones – alongside 25% of the world's population – to own a fridge full of food, clothes on my back and a roof over my head. In the UK alone, there were over 100,000 homeless children[63] in 2022; a shocking figure that includes the sofa surfers of the world – the kids that might sleep on someone's settee and then go on to another 'friend' and sleep there – that we don't consider to be homeless because they're not physically sleeping on the street. But they are homeless and extremely vulnerable, relying on the kindness of human beings who don't always turn out to be that kind, if you know what I mean.

I created an annual charity event called CEO Sleepout about a decade ago, raising money for Action for Children and for six years we got chief executives from leading companies like ITN, Dell UK and Barclays Investment Banking Division to sleep over in Paternoster Square in front of St. Paul's and the London Stock Exchange for one night. During the night it's almost impossible to get any sleep because you've got foxes the size of dogs running around the centre of London, street cleaners and big trucks coming through and a constant stream of worries and feelings of vulnerability. But we raised a quarter of a million pounds every year for homeless children so it was worth every minute.

EXIT SIGNS

I remember one CEO turning to me at 5 am having spent an arduous night on the cobblestones of London and saying he now understood what it felt like to be homeless. And I said, well, yeah, you kind of do and you kind of don't because you've experienced the physical and emotional discomfort, but you were able to endure it because you knew that it was a one-off, knowing that in the morning you would be free to take off, grab a shower and some food and head back to the office. Whereas these guys have no exit strategy or inner voice telling them: if I just hold on for one day, or three days or a week this is going to be over. The demoralisation of that feeling kills all the optimism and energy and everything else. They are existing in a hopeless environment that's never-ending. Any challenge in life is much easier to endure if you have sight of the exit.

At the South Pole we trekked for days through blue skies and blizzards at the mercy of a compass, our fatigue and our wits. Just when I was starting to wonder if there was ever going to be an end in sight, the research station finally appeared on the horizon, boosting our spirits and optimism to see this through. Suddenly, the challenge of three more days walking on very low reserves felt much easier to endure because we had a view of our exit.

Getting a sense of what homelessness is led me to commit to supporting a range of charities that protect, empower and educate children across the globe, including The Lewis Moody Foundation, The Prince's Trust, and The British Asian Trust, to name but a few. Whether that's donating money, time or business expertise, I'm passionate about enabling people to break out of misery and oppression, get their lives back on track and create the future they desire, whether there's an exit sign or not.

Work

HACKATHON HIGHWAYS

If the idea of trekking across Antarctica in sub-zero temperatures doesn't exactly float your boat but you do feel ready to set yourself and others on a life changing path, hackathons provide the perfect opportunity to practice 'everyday' philanthropy and make your own contribution to solving some of the world's biggest issues. It's about bringing compassion, the right mindset and a variety of skills and expertise to the table and acting collectively to bring about social change.

Originally designed to attract programmers and coders to focus on software-based solutions, hackathons provide a fast track to innovation for charities too. These short events lasting just a day or a weekend quickly crowdsource digital ideas and solutions. The word 'hackathon' is a mashup of the words 'hack' (exploratory programming) and 'marathon' *and* blends some of the key ingredients in my life, love and work recipe: technology, entrepreneurship, personal challenge, innovation and collaboration.

During a hackathon, people with a range of skill sets come together to literally hack away at age-old problems such as homelessness and poverty in order to find new technology-enabled solutions. This could be a website, mobile app or a robot. Looking to the future, hackathons could be a game changer for charities and a great investment for philanthropists. Not only are they an original and effective way to find innovative solutions to real-world problems within a set timeframe, they're also cost-effective, foster creativity and offer an opportunity to learn from third party organisations.

DUTY OF CARE

The power of a philanthropic alliance cannot be underestimated to solve the problems of the world, to fight pandemics and overcome future health crises. Unencumbered by the burdens of political bureaucracy or financial motivations, philanthropists have the benefit of agility. Where businesses and governments are answerable to shareholders or voters, philanthropists can move quickly and effectively. Driven by a sense of altruism, these financial first responders are free to plough their resources into funding long-term solutions to seemingly impossible societal problems that align with their personal values and vision without the pressure from other stakeholders. True philanthropy is about effecting long-term social change with no expectation of financial gain. Just like any early start-up, it's about facilitating a grassroots idea to grow and flourish through faith and finance. I guess that's why it's always appealed to me.

Similarly, Corporate Social Responsibility (CSR) is all about shared value creation and giving back. It encompasses the many ways that businesses can divert resources to create benefit for their customers, employees, stakeholders and the communities in which they operate, whether that's through philanthropy – donations of money or time – advocacy or specific corporate social responsibility programmes.

These days, true community and philanthropy engagement should be a core business issue. The most successful businesses will be the ones that actively and authentically engage with important local or global issues however tough the going gets. Like an experienced skipper, business leaders carry a duty of care to ensure the safety of the vessel and all on board. But this extends to the emotional and physical wellbeing of all crew members. My story of the Redbus fire should leave you in no doubt that loyalty is the lifeblood of business. But it's a two-way street. The loyalty must be returned so meaningful CSR will keep businesses fit to weather storms and fight fires in a volatile world. When businesses give back, everybody wins!

Prosper

FINDING YOUR 45º

"Be the change you seek."

MAHATMA GANDHI

Historically, pandemics and plagues have led to ground-breaking leaps forward in literature and science. Shakespeare used a shutdown of theatres to write some of his best poetry, and during The Great Plague in the 1600s, Sir Isaac Newton used his time in social isolation to sit near an apple tree and unlock a fundamental law of physics, gravity![64] As you step back and explore what matters most to you in the wake of the pandemic, what will be your leap forward? How will you develop your own brand of philanthropy?

If you are having a really difficult time, there is always someone who is having an even tougher time. It's all relative so don't see this as a reason to dismiss your troubles; they are important and valid. But actually focusing on trying to solve someone else's problems might be one way of unlocking your own way forward. A very small change in attitude, behaviour or habit can lead to great changes.

LIVE: BREAK IT DOWN

When you are stuck in the blizzards of life, it's hard to see anything at all, let alone a way through! These high-stakes moments require courage, confidence, and clarity, to make a commitment and stick to it. Because, until you are committed, there is always hesitancy, the chance to draw back, ineffectiveness. When it comes to acts of initiative and creation, there is one elementary truth, the ignorance of which kills countless ideas and splendid plans: that the moment one definitely commits oneself, providence moves too.

At that moment, all sorts of things occur to help you that would never otherwise have occurred. A whole stream of events issue from the decision, with all manner of unforeseen incidents, meetings, and material assistance falling into your favour, which you could never have dreamed would come your way. I have learned a deep respect for one of Goethe's couplets:

'Whatever you can do or dream you can, begin it.
Boldness has genius, power and magic in it.
Begin it now.'

W.H. Murray from *The Scottish Himalayan*
Expedition **and Johann Wolfgang von Goethe**

There's a story by WH Murray about climbers on Everest who get to a point between camps when a storm comes in. They are faced with a dilemma: whether to walk back a short distance through the path of a storm to where they just were or push on into the unknown towards the next camp. There is no perfect solution at this point, both directions are fraught with danger but are safer than staying put. They make a decision, and then a series of fortunes fall their way as a result. Like when they come to a crevasse and then a mini avalanche fills it up with snow so they can walk across. Anyway, things turned out well for the climbers.

Never underestimate your body's inherent capacity for endurance, way beyond the mind's capability of understanding it. The problem is that your mind often gets in the way. Perhaps you are in a place in your life where you can relate to that feeling of being in a hopeless environment of never ending where the exit point is never going to come. In fact, your exit point is right in front of you – it's the point at which you commit to a decision to move forward and make a change. As soon as you move through the clouds and chaos of your mind's chatter and out the other side, things will get a lot clearer. Quick, fearless action. Be the change you seek. And let providence in.

LOVE: OPEN UP

For hackathons to be effective they need lots of different people with different skills. In the same way that charity starts at home or work, it also starts within us. The best way we can give back in life, love and work is to spark innovation and creativity within ourselves and others; a 'personal hackathon'. Why not gather a group of similarly minded people, friends, colleagues and dedicate a day to maximising your productivity and boosting your skillset every month or quarter? The possibilities are limitless.

You could use the time to advance an outstanding work project, start a side hustle, or write out a list of life goals or community issues and begin to tackle them. You will suddenly rediscover or find new talents and gifts that you use to make a real difference, and these are the most charitable contributions you can make. Alternatively, plan and run a hackathon at work to fuel ideas and solve problems through bigger picture thinking.[65]

WORK: BE EVER-READY

Ever considered securing a non-Executive Director or Trustee role? If not, why not? This is an invaluable opportunity to contribute your skills and expertise to a worthwhile cause and inject a bit of meaning and purpose to your work as well as taking it in a new and exciting direction. It could be the boost you need if your spirits are flagging.

You might have thought of the idea but dismissed it because you don't think you are high enough up the ladder yet. Don't worry, you don't need to be a senior manager or director to be a NED or trustee. Also, it can be easier to secure the role whilst you're still working, as many organisations want current, operational, hands-on experience. Charities, non-profits and schools will value new and younger perspectives to get smarter in a digital-first world. This might be absolutely the right time to take your place at the board table. To get started, complete the points below:

Do a career inventory: What skills would you like to bring to the table and which would you like to deepen?

Research the roles: Find out what being a NED or a Trustee involves.[66]

Ask others about their experiences: Reach out to people you know in NED and charity trustee positions for advice and information.

Be aware of your legal responsibilities, and don't be afraid to ask questions.[67]

Familiarise yourself with the organisation and build relationships early: This will help you to fully understand the culture and business model and become more confident challenging the status quo.

If you would like to explore the world of philanthropy more generally there are some great podcasts out there offering a deep dive into the lives and work of inspiring and visionary leaders working to change minds and move money to address some of the most critical issues of our time. Have a listen to 'The Road to Philanthropy' by Gary S. Cohn or 'Untapped Philanthropy' and more.[68]

CHAPTER 8

CULTURE

*"Clouds come floating into my life, no longer
to carry rain or usher storm, but to add
colour to my sunset sky."*

RABINDRANATH TAGORE

For a country steeped in cultural heritage, the UK has experienced one culture shock after another over the last few years. First it was Brexit, then the Covid-19 pandemic and now rising inflation impacting on our lives and forcing us to focus on only what we need, rather than what we want to experience to feed our hearts and minds. Living in a 'perma-crisis' has meant that pubs, restaurants, cinemas, theatres, stadiums, galleries and many more entertainment and arts venues have been knocked back and have been feeling the pressure to find their feet again. It's important for our mental health to reflect and remember that tough times don't last forever. The word culture comes from the Latin *colere* which means *'to tend to the earth and grow'*,[69] or to cultivate, nurture and promote growth.

This chapter is about the many ways in which you can flex and adapt your own sense of culture to tend to your mind and grow and thrive in the midst of any crisis.

Live

EPIC-CENTRES

London is the epicentre of my cultural identity, despite having lived in different cities and countries across the world. In addition to my early years in Southern Africa, I worked for eleven years in France, three years in Copenhagen and two years in Frankfurt. I hold board seats in multiple continents and I travelled all over the world for business regularly before Covid hit. Throughout all the storms of life, London has always been my safe harbour. On my return from living in Europe, I remember making a trip out to Guy's Hospital, which now stands in the shadows of the magnificent Shard building. My boyhood neighbourhood had evolved into a thriving hub of suits and boots overlooked by a shiny skyline of skyscrapers; an architectural uprising that echoes my own story. This heart of Bermondsey – where I was born and where my grandmother died – means so much to me that I came full circle and moved into an old rectory, no more than 50 yards from where I used to live. It's where I feel most at home.

Just like London was the epicentre for the war on Covid-19 for a time, it was also the epicentre of a World War Two German bombing campaign that unleashed hell on London and other cities in the United Kingdom during 1940 and 1941. The bombing went on for months, sometimes by day, always by night. Hundreds of people were killed each night. If a bomb happened to strike an underground shelter it could take out dozens in one hit. And yet when their backs were to the wall, Londoners had the last laugh. In fact, during the Blitz, spirits were highest in the most badly hit places. As diarist Phyllis Warner wrote as she explained how so many people felt: 'Finding we can take it is a great relief to most of us.'[70]

This cultural British role modelling of resilience, the 'Keep Calm and Carry On' or 'Blitz Spirit' attitude,[71] is immortalised in the view across to St Paul's from Guy's Hospital, which always reminds me of those sepia images of war-torn London after the Blitz. In the photos, everything has been decimated but St Paul's rises resolutely from the ashes, untouched, stalwart. This building represents the cultural solidarity and community spirit of a city that takes it on the chin. In moments of crisis, I often ground myself by visualising that iconic London cityscape and draw renewed resilience and hope from those empowering cultural landmarks. Buildings old and new that represent the passage of time and our ancestors who lived, loved and worked valiantly through the storms of yesterday.

CULTURAL FAITH

My cultural concoction of home and city, family, food, drink, film and television, travel, the arts, sport and so much more: these are the things that feed my soul, uplift my heart and make me feel better at the end of tough days and weeks. Similar to that feeling I get when I observe the London cityscape, experiencing culture helps me to get things in perspective and liberates me from the stresses and strains of everyday life. This is why it's so important to feed ourselves culturally as well as practically and logically through meeting our mental and physical needs, and we don't need to spend money to do this, culture truly is all around us. By stopping work dominating everything, particularly during tough times, and by consciously giving ourselves a little time to meet our more emotional, creative and holistic needs, we can live with a healthier mindset and experience a more well-rounded, happier lifestyle.

WHAT DOES CULTURE MEAN TO YOU?

Like a faith, culture is highly individual but means many things to many people, and the two concepts can be inextricably bound. Culture can be as simple as what you choose to eat, what you wear and how you wear it. Your language and the way you express yourself, what you believe is right or wrong, how you sit at the table, how you greet visitors, how you behave with loved ones. Culture is also how you choose to spend your spare time and who you choose to share it with; whether that's an annual calendar of festivals, taking part in or watching sports, music, dance, theatre, arts events, gallery openings, which books you read, films you love, or even simply what you watch on the television each night.

Like a faith, your cultural landscape is continually changing and being tested, just as the waves have shaped the land since the beginning of time. But it's hard to believe in anything in the face of continuous change and adversity. The temptation is to give up or just desperately cling to everything you think you know, however strong the winds of change are blowing. But I urge you to keep the faith, and take that leap of faith, even when you have no grounds to do so, to reach new heights of cultural satisfaction that will help you to live, love and work in a way that feels good.

Love

CURB YOUR ENTHUSIASM

Experiencing culture, whether it's through visiting a museum, watching a sports match in a stadium or attending the theatre, can do so much for our mental and physical health. The appreciation of art, theatre, food, music, history and more allows us to feel love and boosts our endorphins in all sorts of ways. Cultural enjoyment provides a sense of belonging and companionship as we enjoy it, shoulder to shoulder, with friends, family and other like-minded enthusiasts. Unfortunately, this also provided the perfect conditions for a new virus to spread uncontrollably.

Never before was our cultural enthusiasm so severely curbed when stadiums, galleries, museums, world heritage sites, theatres, nightclubs, concert halls and restaurants closed across the world during March 2020. Saturday night plans to sit inside a musty room and share a grubby glass of beer with friends were shelved as our beloved pubs in the UK shut their doors. This was unprecedented. Even Churchill kept pubs open throughout two world wars because he believed a healthy beer supply was good for morale!

Before the pandemic there was barely a weekend when there wasn't some sort of live sporting coverage blaring out from stadiums and screens in pubs, bars and living rooms across the country. Once we were locked down though, and as we waited for a vaccine in order to have our freedom back, the stadium lights went out and the crowds fell quiet. Worldwide and at all levels, just about any kind of sport was shut down, games were cancelled and seasons were postponed. UK sports fans, athletes and coaches were resigned to their sofas and only able to relive some nostalgic TV sporting moments, like Euro 96 and the 2012 London Olympics, and even a simulated version of the Grand National attracted over 5 million viewers.[72]

Thanks to technology, however, museums and galleries quickly pivoted to virtual tours and online access to archives. From interactive 360-degree videos and full walk-around tours with voiceover descriptions to slideshows with zoomable photos, people could suddenly get closer to the real deal than they ever could as museum goers. For example, The British Museum's cutting-edge partnership with Google Art and Culture meant that every person on the planet could virtually walk around the British Museum as if it were their own private collection and explore the world in their own way.[73]

Musicians and bands went online and intimate, using live social media streams, music lessons and DJ sets from their bedrooms. From Broadway to the West End and Shakespeare's Globe, theatres locally, nationally and globally opened up their archives, streaming some of the world's best plays and musicals straight into our living rooms.[74]

Thankfully the darkness was temporary and stadiums re-opened, the actors returned to the stage and fans and audiences made their gradual return. It's a reassuring reminder that it will take much more than a pandemic to keep our culture from bouncing back.

A WHOLE NEW BALL GAME

As we reflect on the role technology played in keeping us liberated and connected to our cultural pleasures during the pandemic, it's clear that tech will play a big role in the sporting world in the years to come. It already does with the advent of innovations like VAR, the video assisted referee, as we will find sports to be more and more integrated with tech to offer a truly personal and immersive experience, whether we choose to sit in a stadium or not.

More than ever before, the sports industry has been challenged to invest in and think creatively about new ways to support and expand the remote fan experience to strengthen engagement, build brand value, and drive revenue growth for all sport related business. Virtual reality, artificial intelligence and augmented reality will be critical in defining the future of the sports fan experience and how they engage in real time. These emerging technologies really are proving they have the capacity to deliver satisfying, hyper personalised and multi-layered experiences that give the fans what they want, when they want it and wherever they want it. Whether it's the chance to sit in a virtual courtside seat, follow a particular player at any given point during the game or connect with other fans and game information via multiple devices, video conferencing apps and social streams, technology will help us direct the experience we want and keep us well and truly up to speed with our rapidly evolving world and cultural tastes.

Work

IN THE DEEP END

The pandemic has shown that the strongest cultures grow and thrive during times of great change. At work, during the actual action of learning to change, people become less frightened and deal with tasks they didn't even know they could deal with; it's fear of the unknown that is the problem. The shared challenges mean that everyone in a given situation can experience the same interpretation of pain, risk, success, challenge, teamwork. Creating a real shared ethos and culture.

Back in 2006, I wanted to create an experience that would help my newly merged team convert their fearfulness into fearlessness – something that would instil fear in them but then show them that their fear was unfounded. So I took them off to swim with sharks. Face to face with an icon of danger. This would be confronting fear by being thrown in at the deep end. Despite the palpable terror, in the end everyone swam – everyone except one person.

At dinner afterwards, I asked everyone for their feedback. Everyone admitted to having felt terrified about what was in store, even though the instructors did their best to reassure them. Once they were on the seabed, they still felt terrified being eye to eye with three-metre-long hammerheads and tiger sharks, but this was nowhere near as terrifying as the anticipation and apprehension back on the boat. Once they realised that the sharks were swimming up to them out of curiosity rather than hunger – just like the instructors had said they would – they were able to adjust their expectations and embrace the moment.

'And what did you feel when you came out?' I asked.

'It was a life-changing experience.' 'I was overcome. I dealt with something that I didn't even know was an issue.'

For some it was simply life changing. For others it helped them deal with issues that they didn't even realise they needed to deal with. Most revealing of all though was the one colleague who had not swum with the sharks. He felt deep regret and a sense of alienation because he could not share the experience with the others.

My decision to take the team swimming with sharks was not me being ruthless, macho or gimmicky. It was a genuine intention to make a profound impact on the people who took part and contribute to the growth of a newly formed ethos and culture built upon this unique and shared experience.

Dealing with fear doesn't mean denying that fear exists. But to progress, grow and thrive, you have to learn to be able to channel the fear and make that change from fearful to fearless.

TEAMWORK MAKES THE DREAM WORK

You don't always need to go to the extreme, but businesses that focus on fostering a culture of compassion by encouraging colleagues to work together to support each other will flourish in our turbulent new normal.

This takes me back to when I was young and my sister told me one of Aesop's Tales about the North Wind and the Sun. In the story the sun and the wind have a bet about a man below them with his coat on. The wind says to the sun, 'I reckon I can get this guy's coat off.' So the wind starts blowing as hard as he can, and of course the harder it blows, the tighter this man wraps his coat around him. Then the sun has a go, sending down his strongest rays. The man immediately takes his coat off because he feels so warm, proving the sun's wise theory that: 'Gentleness and kind persuasion win where force and bluster fail'.[75]

In these volatile times, it's more important than ever that we become spreaders of happiness; to cultivate a culture of teamwork and compassion that transcends any measure of pain and hardship that the world may have in store for us both now and into the future. Think about it. Happiness makes us so much more productive. I shiver at the thought of how many hours and how much energy I've wasted at work, and at home on unnecessary conflict, which quite frankly has turned out to be 'bluster'. In strong team cultures, it's clear that people care about one another's wellbeing, they look out for one another and pick up the slack for one another. So why not at work too? Teamwork should be endemic within the culture of workplaces and business settings. This shared experience is what energises you and empowers you to keep marching forward – no matter how tough the terrain may be.

Prosper

FINDING YOUR 45º

*"The brightest thunder-bolt is elicited
from the darkest storm."*

CHARLES CALEB COLTON

There is a tradition in theatre that whenever the building lies empty, one 'ghost light' is left on. It's basically a lamp that keeps the stage safely lit to avoid anyone tumbling into the orchestra pit when everything gets powered off at the end of the night. Although superstition has it that the light means ghosts can have their turn on stage when no-one else is about, so they don't end up causing havoc during the shows!

During lockdown 'ghost lights' were not just lit in theatres but in museums, galleries, concert halls and cinemas across the world. Rather than a sign of hopelessness, the light became a blazing beacon of hope in the storm, like a lighthouse guiding ships to safety; a sign that culture was very much open for business, just with the help of some creative thinking and technology.

If you are feeling completely in the dark at the moment, here are some ways to illuminate your inner 'ghost light', reawaken your cultural mindset and beam out your rays of creativity and wisdom to guide others through their storms:

LIVE: BREAK IT DOWN

In life there are two types of people, 'Radiators' and 'Drains'. 'Radiators' are the people who radiate warmth – if you've got any radiators in your life, then snuggle up to them. They naturally make people feel good about themselves. Like the sun's rays, they give out warmth, energy and enthusiasm. Their cups are always half full. 'Drains', on the other hand, do what they say on the tin. Like energy vampires, they literally suck the energy out of you. They're the ones that leave you feeling small, flat and run down. Like those times when you started off a conversation in a bright and cheery way and you came away from it feeling negative and frustrated, or even cranky and irritable. Be honest now. Which one are you? Do you find yourself flipping between the two? If you have Drain-like moments, try to catch yourself in the moment, turn it around and look for the bright side. Try to take responsibility for your behaviour by not acting like a drain or allowing yourself to be drained. Life's too short for drains. The more you can train yourself to project warmth and light, the more you will get it back in return from others, which will help healthy, happy cultures to flourish at work and at home.

LOVE: OPEN UP

I've always said that by setting aside a little time in your day it's possible to show how much you appreciate the people you live and work with; a simple expression that says way more than a bunch of flowers or a box of chocolates. I remember at one management get-together in Tenerife, I wound up the day's proceedings by saying to the team, 'I would like all of you, every morning before 12 o'clock until the end of this month, to send a message to someone in this room with a "thank you" for something they have done, and make sure you copy everybody else in.' They thought I was nuts of course, but the habit caught on and it was massively uplifting. People were saying, 'I didn't even realise you knew I did that. I didn't know you appreciated me.' And others said, 'She did that for you? Could you do that for me too?' Nowadays there are brilliant digital platforms and employee engagement tools like Kudos,[76] that enable quick and easy shout-outs; radiating warmth and happiness at the click of a button.

The same goes for your culture outside of work. It's so important to treat our family and our friends with the same love and respect that we do our colleagues. Rather than dividing up our time and energy, trying to keep the two things separate, we can multiply our efforts and channel them into one shared culture, ethos and experience where everyone feels valued.

WORK: BE EVER-READY

The challenges of our increasingly volatile world, including fears over new illnesses and the rising cost of living, may be fuelling stress in your workplace to the point that it's affecting mental health and performance. In a world where people want to feel valued and recognised and employers want to protect their valued business drivers, creating a culture of trust at every level of your organisation is the first step towards having a conversation about financial wellbeing. Here are some ways you can start to approach the delicate and emotional topic with your teams, or advise colleagues to do the same:

Use the right tools: With huge variations in levels of financial literacy and everyone being affected by personal or global crises differently, it's important to gain an insight into what people might already know and also what they might need. Adopting a data-driven approach using tools such as listening exercises, surveys and focus groups to collect information directly from employees can be a great way to find out how much they know, what steps they can take and how comfortable they feel about addressing financial concerns.

Build a clear and well-structured strategy: Use employee feedback to set out specific objectives of how you want to support them with valuable but not costly benefits. This could include financial wellbeing education, wellbeing apps, internal wellbeing champion schemes, awareness raising programmes and signposting people to relevant and specialist support systems.

Adopt simple, inclusive messaging: Avoid jargon-heavy or trivial communication to achieve clarity and impact. Find out how your people like to receive messages. Reaching out via a text, email or on a video conferencing call might feel more comfortable for some. Whereas others may respond better to face to face, more human interactions.

Lead by example: Conversations about money can lead to deep-seated emotional responses and building a culture of trust is one of the best ways of normalising those conversations.

CHAPTER 9

ENVIRONMENT

The great challenge of this century is undoubtedly how we meet the needs of all, within the means of a rapidly changing planet. Finding a balance between sustainability, social justice and quality of life requires far-reaching decisions and choices. Once these have been made, using smart technologies to realise them creates effective solutions.

Covid-19 thrust the world into its greatest experiment yet, as we grappled with the challenge of how to revert to business as usual within the grip of a global pandemic. Before we knew it, living, loving and working online had become commonplace. Suddenly, everything we thought was impossible became possible because it had to. This just goes to show what joined up society can achieve when it needs to! It was a great lesson to all, but let's not stop there.

This chapter is about how technology and big-picture-thinking will help to create a better environment to live, love and work in, no matter where that may be. I suggest ways that you can start playing your part now to create a healthier, fairer and greener world for future generations. It's also about how you can protect your mental health and convert your fears about what the future holds for the planet in an unpredictable world into fearless action.

Live

DIGITAL EQUALITY

Digital equality offers one of the greatest potential global opportunities in terms of making the Internet accessible and affordable for the whole population of the world. In India, as part of the 2022 budget, the Finance Minister recently classified data centres as part of the 'nation's infrastructure',[77] which means that they get the same vital national status and importance as water, gas, and electricity.

When we pivoted to remote working during lockdown it exposed an appalling digital divide that is holding back almost half the planet. Even the wealthiest of nations still struggle to get connected. Shockingly, many homes today do not have the Internet. In this day and age the web can and must be for everyone; no one should be out of reach of high-quality connectivity.

Africa has the lowest number of Internet connections and the highest potential for progress. As non-executive director for Africa's largest data centre company, Teraco, I saw first-hand how a critical backbone of connectivity across the 53 countries accelerated Africa's digital transformation and made the continent healthier, fairer and more prosperous. With major subsea fibre optic cables bringing a never-been-available-before potential for the development of connectivity across the continent, now is the time for big, bold action, which makes Internet connectivity the rule, not the exception across sub-Saharan Africa.

LEVELLING THE FIELD

Why? Because data will help to solve some of the biggest problems facing humanity, such as the scarcity of water and food in developing countries. Projects like Microsoft's 'Farm Beats'[78] could put Africa at the leading edge of global economic and environmental sustainability. This innovative and inclusive approach empowers and enables data-driven farming that works in harmony with the farmer's vast knowledge and intuition with the end goal of increasing farm productivity and reducing costs across the continent.

With the right technology and infrastructure we can level the playing field. And where we can't lay cables, we can use satellites. For example, Bigblu Broadband's[79] sole objective is to provide high-speed broadband via satellite to residents of remote areas who will never see a strand of fibre come into their homes, making the previous geographical, physical constraints of poor connectivity a thing of the past, and setting the stage for a remarkable new normal, not just in how we live, but where we live.

Love

LOVE YOUR PLANET, LOVE YOURSELF

Climate change is the result of long-term changes in temperature and weather patterns over hundreds and thousands of years. But our obsession with burning fossil fuels like natural gas, oil and coal to heat homes, run vehicles, power industry and manufacturing, and provide electricity has accelerated the rate of change. Everything we consume, from the food we eat to the things we buy, to the way we travel, releases greenhouse gases like carbon dioxide into the atmosphere. The gases capture heat from the sun and cause temperatures to rise, also known as global warming or the greenhouse effect.

Extreme weather like hurricanes, floods and tropical storms are the planet's angry response to our greedy guzzling. Unpredictable weather patterns such as temperature and rainfall make it difficult for farmers to maintain and grow crops. In polar regions, the warming global temperatures are melting ice sheets and glaciers, which is causing sea levels to rise and destroying animal habitats.

Russia's invasion of Ukraine added fuel to the fire. As the world's largest exporter of gas turned off its supply to Europe during 2022 it sent the world into an energy crisis like never before. This was yet another reminder to end our reliance on fossil fuels to heat our homes and power our cars once and for all by investing in alternative and proven sources of energy that are clean, accessible, affordable, sustainable, and reliable. After all, if our planet is kind enough to supply us with our food, water and air, it's essential we repay that kindness before it's too late.

HOPE SPRINGS

During the height of the pandemic, when mass movement stalled like never before, grimy Venice canals turned clear and the usually smog-filled skies over Delhi turned blue as the congestion-riddled, pollution-choked streets around the world fell eerily quiet for a time. Cars, buses and trains remained stationary as people turned to cycling during lockdown, for exercise or essential journeys. With the oil industry and airlines on pause, carbon emissions plummeted in April. This showed us that there is much cause for hope, and if we take action now, the effects of climate change could be slowed down or even reversed.

Policies and technology-driven initiatives to harness our plentiful and renewable resources of sun, wind and water to power our industries and reduce air pollution will offer a win-win strategy for both climate and health. Governments and countries that seize this moment to make it easier and safer for people to use cleaner, greener modes of transport and introduce car-free zones, temporary cycle lanes and walk-ways, will not only recover better from the pandemic, they will prosper.

Work

HOME TRUTHS

Working from home was first touted as a solution to traffic congestion back in 1973, by former Nasa engineer Jack Nilles. Titled 'The Telecommunications-Transportation Tradeoff', it hardly flew off the shelves. The limitations of technology didn't help either! The 'personal computer' appeared two years later but it would still take a decade before it was fit for general consumption and supported by the necessary infrastructure. (All thanks to the dawn of the data centre!)

Even though Jack's 'bean' of an idea was in a much better position to flourish by the 1990s, only a small percentage dared to grab hold of the beanstalk. In the end, it took a global pandemic thirty years later to tip the balance, accelerate the transition to remote working and shift attitudes about how the future working environment could be reconfigured.

This unprecedented remote working movement has reworked not just our cultural understanding of a corporate community, but also our very concept of physical reality.

The shift from structured office work to more remote arrangements, has reduced the demand for office space and created distributed, mixed-use working environments in town and city suburbs, which give people greater autonomy over where and indeed how they live.

Hybrid offices of the future could become more campus-like: part coffee shop and bar for spontaneous meetings, hot-desking hubs for organised activities, or libraries for those who need a quiet escape from home. Investment in technology to leverage automated solutions such as online meetings is closing the digital divide, radically reducing physical travel, especially around the traditional daily commute, which is starting to give rise to pedestrianised areas, thus fuelling the growing eco-appetite for walking, cycling and scootering safely.

We now have the chance to reimagine the design and location of our work environments to help rebuild confidence and productivity. Whether you work best from home or the office, the sustainability of businesses will not only depend upon creating cleaner, greener environments, but on keeping hold of good employees, who thrive upon a culture that celebrates choice, voice, health and wellbeing. Many businesses I'm involved with cite the optionality of being based in an office or at home as one of the key criteria new recruits look for, even ahead of salary levels.

RESISTANCE IS FUTILE, RESILIENCE IS KEY

"Achieving a sustainable future is the growth story of our time, and can in fact fuel our post-pandemic recovery in a way that pays dividends for decades to come, but the window for action is rapidly closing. The good news is that, on every pressing issue we face, there are

solutions that are not just available, but increasingly cost effective. A new marshall-like plan for nature, people and planet is urgently needed if we are to align our collective efforts for the highest possible impact, and to save our planet from continued destruction. I trust you will all agree that our children and grandchildren deserve nothing less."

HIS MAJESTY KING CHARLES

It remains to be seen whether Covid-19 or climate change turns out to become the worst crisis of our time, but it may be that in overcoming one, we can overcome all. The resilient actions we take now towards harnessing nature-based solutions and contributing towards a green recovery could shape human existence for generations to come.

For example, we have a rich treasure in the sea and I'm not talking pirates or pearls. In our fight against climate change and environmental damage, seaweed could be our biggest weapon. Beneath the waves, lies a rich, bountiful and sustainable source of food, fuel, fertiliser and even a biodegradable plastic substitute. For a plant that grows one metre in just two days, all efforts are underway to take seaweed farming to the next level.

The North Sea Farmers consortium[80] in The Netherlands has challenged experts, entrepreneurs and energy companies to experiment with growing seaweed in the spaces between offshore wind turbines using floating solar panels.

In Namibia, they are building a $60 million offshore kelp farm[81] to reap the benefits of deeper, more nutrient-rich waters.

If you're ready to embrace the climate challenge and play your part in creating a sustainable future, the possibilities are just like seaweed itself: diverse, abundant, and growing by the day. It's clear that we've reached a pivotal point in climate change so now is the time to grab those possibilities with both hands. As we endure storm after storm, the untapped potential of seaweed is something to feel really optimistic about. The future really does look bright.

Prosper

"There are no passengers on Spaceship Earth.
We are all crew."

MARSHALL MCLUHAN

FINDING YOUR 45º

As this chapter has demonstrated, energy lies at the heart of the climate challenge, but it also lies at the heart of the solution. While the Covid-19 pandemic certainly highlighted the precarious relationship between people and planet, it also demonstrated the power of collective energy when people come together to tackle large, global challenges.

As you continue reprogramming your brain, rebooting to this brave new world and adjusting to your 'new normal', try to notice the silver linings and tune into the exciting opportunities for change ahead. Summon your newfound purpose, energy and self-belief and do all you can – small or big – to steer the planet forwards to a more liveable and sustainable future. Every little effort will count. Not only will this renewed awareness of needing to be more flexible, fearless and adaptable, better prepare you for any other 'new normals' that you may get to experience in your lifetime, you'll also be making a contribution to a healthier, fairer and greener planet for generations to come!

LIVE: BREAK IT DOWN

With fossil fuels, such as coal, oil and gas, accounting for over 75 percent of global greenhouse gas emissions and nearly 90 percent of all carbon dioxide emissions, the science is clear. To avoid the worst impact of climate change, emissions need to be reduced by almost half by 2030 and reach net-zero by 2050.[82]

With work travel the largest source of carbon emissions in the developed world pre-Covid, remote working is a clear winner in the race for decarbonisation, as the dramatic drop in carbon levels during lockdown demonstrated. Having been forced to experiment, businesses must seize this moment to continue pushing forward with carbon reduction to ultimately future-proof operations.

You can help the world transition to net-zero by decarbonizing how you move around and eliminating the carbon-intensive actions from your life that you can: walking or riding a bike instead of driving down the street could save millions of short journeys. Call or use a video conference instead of flying in for a business meeting. Whether you choose to buy an e-scooter to avoid using the tube like I did, or simply dust off your bike and give it a bit of TLC, start reducing your own personal carbon footprint, get healthier and rekindle your fragile relationship with the planet today; whether that's embracing two wheels or two feet!

LOVE: OPEN UP

Whether it's a severe weather forecast or a new bleak report on the future of the planet, it's really easy to let daily social media feeds about the emerging climate crisis and what feels like a continual stream of natural disasters, such as floods, droughts and wildfires in the news, get to you. You are not alone.

In fact, the climate change issues are having such a damaging effect on people's mental health that the American Psychological Association have given it a name: 'climate anxiety', defining it as 'a chronic fear of environmental doom'.[83] Also known as 'eco-distress', it's the feeling of anxiety that more and more people are feeling about the state of the environment, which can manifest as fear, worry, and even anger about the effects of climate change. The immensity of the problem might leave you feeling overwhelmed, disempowered, and sometimes guilty about the role you may have played in causing it. You might find yourself asking, what can one person possibly do about such a giant issue? Or you might feel completely frustrated about the inaction you witness around you, which then in turn triggers physical and emotional symptoms of anxiety, e.g. sweaty palms, a racing heart, a tightening in the chest or simply worry, increased irritability, difficulty concentrating, restless sleep and anger.

The good news is there are some great tools out there to help you manage your feelings, stay grounded and convert your fear into action.

The everyday mindfulness and meditation app, Headspace, has some great suggestions on how to combine mindfulness techniques with more proactive life choices, like campaigning to make a difference to overcome climate anxiety.[84]

Alternatively, download the Hazel app[85] to take responsibility for your own carbon footprint and ease your climate guilt, for less than your monthly Netflix subscription. The app calculates the environmental cost or carbon generated from the everyday activities that you can't eliminate from your life, e.g. a tank of gas, an upcoming flight or your monthly electrical use. Then, for each pound of carbon you generate, it enables you to fund the removal of the equivalent amount of carbon from the atmosphere via one of their carbon removal projects. If everyone did this, we'd start reversing climate change. So start leading change!

WORK: BE EVER-READY

With more people opting for flexible working from home that enables a much healthier and happier work life integration, think about choosing a work environment that truly sets you up for success in life and join the growing trend towards working from holiday.

You might think, hang on, but isn't a holiday about setting your out of office and having a complete switch off from work? Well, it is to a point, but then you get that nagging feeling in the pit of your stomach towards the end about the prospect of returning to an inbox full of emails and meeting requests.

Explore the benefits of replicating the work you would otherwise be doing at your desk at home while sitting on a sun-drenched beach in Spain. You could plan an hour or two at the beginning or end of each day or every other day to keep on top of the mounting workload or even tag on remote working days at the start or end of a trip to extend your holiday and make the most of your time away.

Revealingly, 39% of UK adults worked from holiday in 2022, with 28% saying that it helped them feel more positively about their workplace.[86] Let's face it, we are all better versions of ourselves in a holiday environment, which positively impacts on our relationships with the family and friends there with us, so why not try it?

If you have already developed a taste for working from home, then why not take it one step further? Consider renting out your house, ditch the office completely and make a completely new holistic and eco-friendly lifestyle choice by becoming a digital, global nomad with complete location independence, where travel remains the ultimate aspiration.

All you will need is a laptop and a co-working space, public library or coffee shop with a decent Internet signal to work from wherever you happen to be in the world. In the wake of the pandemic, many countries are now starting to recognise the need for digital nomad or remote work visas to entice foreigners to come and live, work and contribute to their economies to make up for lost tourism revenue, so do your research.[87]

You will also be doing your bit for the environment by travelling with the bare minimum and reducing your carbon footprint. Your ability to adapt with greater confidence and control to any environment or situation will enable you to break free from limiting belief and patterns of thought and head out on a new tangent. This really is the ultimate in life, love and work integration, underpinned by technology!

AFTERWORD

Life is tough… you pay taxes and then you die.

Is that it?

It can sometimes feel like the world is conspiring against us and work environments seem to be getting tougher by the day.

A US tech firm recently fired people without warning while they were onboarding newcomers! Imagine it's your first day on the job. You eat the free biscuits, work out where the bathrooms are, get all your passwords sorted out, and while you're having your induction speech the guy giving it is fired right in front of you while he's praising the culture of the company!

These days, **there's no such thing** as a steady job in technology. I was chatting to a friend who, like me, works with multiple organisations, and he said his daughter and two sons had each started their own businesses, his lawyer wife had retired but started a high-end dog-walking company. He said he didn't actually know anyone that had a 'normal' or 'traditional' job.

The scaremongers of yesteryear said that robots and computers would create massive unemployment, but the reality is that some jobs have disappeared but millions more jobs have been created by technology. But it's not easy...

In the video-game industry, employers are using scare tactics to make already overworked employees meet new deadlines and cut costs. 'The ball is in your court,' Ubisoft's CEO recently said in a tone-deaf speech to staffers – many of whom are pulling 60-to-100-hour work weeks to create the 983rd iteration of *Assassin's Creed*. As Lionel notes, Ubisoft's dilemma reflects poor decisions by the company, not the workers. No wonder they're considering a strike.

Allison Schrager argues Gen-Z workers should try harder to make their bosses like them. But Andrea Felsted suggests upper management can do its part by re-evaluating its approach to workplace wellness, especially at a time when mental-health struggles are on the rise.

A free slice of cake never hurts the mood and can even lure workers back to the office, Andrea writes. But perks of the snacking variety are no substitute for a pay raise. Japan's government understands this and is pushing infamously stingy Japanese companies to open their wallets, Gearoid Reidy explains. At the moment, they don't even reward job-changers.

If employers don't meet workers at least halfway then we may see more reactions like Amazon software engineer Ankali Tewani's tongue-in-cheek suggestion that people be strategically terrible at their jobs: 'If you build complex systems that no one understands and you have horrible documentation, then they're not going to fire you. They need you to run things! But if you're a good engineer and you build simple systems that everyone understands, then you are replaceable and you're getting laid off.' Something's got to give.

Perhaps the lone bright spot in Big Tech is in the dark. The sleep-tech industry wants to capitalise on your nightmares by tracking your 'sleep performance' through a variety of new-fangled gadgets. 'The most restful pastime humans can enjoy is starting to look like a competitive sport,' Tim Culpan writes, with everyone from Garmin to Apple trying to get into bed with you. But after they start tracking your REM, there's little the device can do to improve the quality of your sleep. And in some instances, wearables do more harm than help.

Sleep coaches – a real career that exists – are also working hard to get you more shut-eye. There are online courses. Slumber sessions. Some startups even send you mail-order mattresses, fully equipped with automatically adjusting air chambers or dynamic hot/cool water tubes. But whether these guides and gadgets can actually deliver results is a bedtime story for another day.

Ultimately, remember this: life is not a rehearsal. Every day that passes is a day less on earth that you have to live, love work and prosper. Challenges in all aspects of life are inevitable and in a way create the reference points for us to measure success and happiness. You have to experience the downs to appreciate the highs. Think of life as a heart monitor. Without the ups and downs, a straight line means we are dead!

Embrace challenges like they are airline tickets to your vacation. No-one likes to buy them but when we step off the plane it's all worth it!

REFERENCES

www.thetimes.co.uk/article/telecity

https://www.imdb.com/title/tt0128853/

Introduction

https://www.who.int/dg/speeches
https://www.gov.uk/government/speeches/pm-address-to-the-nation-on-coronavirus-23-march-2020
https://www.who.int/dg/speeches/detail/who-director-general-s-opening-remarks-at-the-media-briefing-on-covid-19---3-march-2020
https://www.gov.uk/government/publications/staying-alert-and-safe-social-distancing/staying-alert-and-safe-social-distancing#:~:text=You%20should%20keep%20two%20metres,a%20private%20vehicle%20where%20possible.
https://dangerousthings.com/about-implants/
https://en.wikipedia.org/wiki/The_Great_Escape_(film)
https://news.sky.com/story/coronavirus-what-might-our-new-normal-look-like-when-the-uk-lockdown-is-eased-11979256

Chapter 1

https://www.telegraph.co.uk/news/2020/04/09/ae-attendances-lowest-point-since-records-began-amid-coronavirus/
https://en.wikipedia.org/wiki/Black_Mirror
https://web.stanford.edu/~mrosenfe/Rosenfeld_et_al_Disintermediating_Friends.pdf
https://techcrunch.com/2020/06/30/global-app-revenue-jumps-to-50b-in-the-first-half-of-2020-in-part-due-to-covid-19-impacts
https://www.bbc.co.uk/news/business-52743454

https://www.onlinepersonalswatch.com/news/2020/06/the-growth-stages-of-the-Internet-dating-industry.html
https://en.wikipedia.org/wiki/Zoom_Video_Communications
https://www.independent.co.uk/life-style/royal-family/queen-harry-meghan-royal-family-william-kate-lockdown-zoom-b598359.html
https://www.bbc.co.uk/news/uk-england-london-36272893
https://www.bbc.co.uk/programmes/m000hkb3
https://www.telegraph.co.uk/business/2016/05/27/the-best-quotes-to-help-you-find-business-success/facebook-ceo-mark-zuckerberg-speaks-at-a-facebook-innovation-hub/
https://www.theguardian.com/media/video/2017/mar/10/bbc-correspondent-interrupted-by-his-children-live-on-air-video
https://uk.room.com/products/room-privacy-booth
https://aquietrefuge.com/make-soundproof-booth/

Chapter 2

https://www.reuters.com/article/us-health-coronavirus-trump-disinfectant/trumps-disinfectant-ideas-horrify-doctors-and-academics-idUSKCN2261N7
https://globalnews.ca/news/6871768/coronavirus-donald-trump-disinfectant-poison/
https://www.theguardian.com/media/mind-your-language/2014/sep/26/mind-your-language-war-words
https://public.oed.com/blog/the-language-of-covid-19/
https://www.forbes.com/sites/trello/2019/10/08/5-leadership-skills-you-can-develop-in-the-mountains/?sh=70a940ad4fbf
https://www.theguardian.com/world/2020/apr/17/prince-william-pays-tribute-to-war-veteran-tom-moore-who-raised-millions-for-nhs
https://slack.com/intl/en-gb/
https://bigblu.co.uk/satellite-Internet/

Chapter 3

https://www.england.nhs.uk/wp-content/uploads/2014/10/5yfv-web.pdf
https://employeebenefits.co.uk/fujitsu-remote-working-80000-employees/
https://www.thetimes.co.uk/article/pwc-under-fire-for-tech-that-keeps-home-working-staff-under-surveillance-t2h870dxg
https://en.wikipedia.org/wiki/Dodo
https://uk.burberry.com/burberry-supports-the-fight-against-covid-19/
https://www.brewdog.com/blog/business-as-a-force-for-good
https://www.mckinsey.com/business-functions/organization/our-insights/ready-set-go-reinventing-the-organization-for-speed-in-the-post-covid-19-era

Chapter 4

https://www.ecnmy.org/learn/you/
https://d25d2506sfb94s.cloudfront.net/cumulus_uploads/document/5tw8cdop65/RethinkingEconomicsResults_160229_Media&Economics_w.pdf
https://www.ecnmy.org/wp-content/uploads/2017/11/Exploring-How-People-Feel-About-Economics-Research-Report-2017-ecnmy.org_.pdf/
https://www.bankofengland.co.uk/knowledgebank/what-is-money
https://www.apple.com/uk/apple-pay/
https://www.gov.uk/government/news/rishis-plan-for-jobs-will-help-britain-bounce-back
https://www.bbc.co.uk/news/business-51490893
https://www.imdb.com/title/tt0038650/
https://www.telegraph.co.uk/business/2020/04/14/transitioned-retail-analyst-tesco-worker/
https://www.telegraph.co.uk/royal-family/2020/05/18/pick-britain-prince-charles-urges-new-land-army-take-hard-graft/
https://www.bbc.co.uk/news/uk-england-hereford-worcester-53381802
https://www.ft.com/content/eaaf12e8-907a-11ea-bc44-dbf6756c871a
https://www.dezeen.com/2018/06/07/nino-robotic-bartender-can-make-any-drink-in-seconds/
https://www.weforum.org/agenda/2020/05/robots-coronavirus-crisis/
https://www.ft.com/content/c9adddb6-e460-11e9-b8e0-026e07cbe5b4
https://blog.mywallst.com/shopify-set-for-a-big-2020/
https://www.forbes.com/sites/jaimecatmull/2019/10/07/the-15-best-investment-apps-for-everyday-investors/#7e9d3c1e145b
https://www.thisismoney.co.uk/money/investing/article-6929525/The-trendy-apps-turn-change-cup-coffee-nice-little-nest-egg.html
https://www.entrepreneur.com/article/327554
https://www.oberlo.co.uk/blog/side-hustle

Chapter 5

https://www.who.int/docs/default-source/coronaviruse/transcripts/who-audio-emergencies-coronavirus-press-conference-full-08apr2020.pdf?sfvrsn=267145f5_2
https://en.wikipedia.org/wiki/Chaos_engineering#Chaos_Monkey
https://governmentbusiness.co.uk/news/17072020/plan-worst-hope-best-says-johnson
https://www.parliament.uk/about/art-in-parliament/online-exhibitions/parliamentarians/harold-wilson/image-1/
https://www.bbc.co.uk/news/uk-46318565
https://www.bbc.co.uk/news/politics/eu_referendum/results

https://www.telegraph.co.uk/politics/2019/07/25/boris-johnson-used-bumbling-today-looked-totally-transformed/

https://www.bbc.co.uk/news/av/uk-politics-49601128/boris-johnson-i-d-rather-be-dead-in-a-ditch-than-ask-for-brexit-delay

https://time.com/5749478/get-brexit-done-slogan-uk-election/

https://www.economist.com/britain/2020/05/10/boris-johnsons-new-covid-19-campaign-falls-flat

https://www.theguardian.com/politics/2020/apr/27/muggers-and-invisible-enemies-how-boris-johnsons-metaphors-reveals-his-thinking

https://www.independent.co.uk/news/uk/politics/boris-johnson-news-coronavirus-update-hospital-discharge-today-a9461461.html

https://www.medrxiv.org/content/10.1101/2020.04.23.20076042v1

https://www.telegraph.co.uk/health-fitness/body/boris-right-time-honest-weight-problem/

https://www.michaeltobin.online/podcast/

https://yougov.co.uk/topics/politics/articles-reports/2020/03/24/how-covid-19-affecting-british-opinions-jobs-and-w

https://iris.paho.org/bitstream/handle/10665.2/52052/Factsheet-infodemic_eng.pdf?sequence=14

https://www.bbc.co.uk/news/world-africa-52544187

https://theconversation.com/coronavirus-there-are-no-miracle-foods-or-diets-that-can-prevent-or-cure-covid-19-136666

https://theconversation.com/conspiracy-theories-about-5g-networks-have-skyrocketed-since-covid-19-139374

https://www.forbes.com/sites/brucelee/2020/04/19/bill-gates-is-now-a-target-of-covid-19-coronavirus-conspiracy-theories/#9d20dc662277

https://theconversation.com/covid19-social-media-both-a-blessing-and-a-curse-during-coronavirus-pandemic-133596

https://edition.cnn.com/2020/02/20/us/coronavirus-racist-attacks-against-asian-americans/index.html

https://www.independent.co.uk/news/world/middle-east/coronavirus-iran-deaths-toxic-methanol-alcohol-fake-news-rumours-a9487801.html

https://www.theguardian.com/us-news/commentisfree/2020/apr/19/trump-is-playing-a-deadly-game-in-deflecting-covid-19-blame-to-china

https://www.independent.co.uk/voices/coronavirus-trump-china-us-cold-war-election-economy-iraq-a9494451.html

https://www.telegraph.co.uk/politics/2020/07/18/boris-johnson-exclusive-interview-will-not-need-another-national/

https://www.bbc.co.uk/news/uk-politics-31049249

https://www.forbes.com/sites/ekaterinawalter/2013/12/30/30-powerful-quotes-on-failure/#acccf8524bd1

https://www.oecd.org/coronavirus/en/

https://www.entrepreneur.com/article/313349

https://theconversation.com/5-ways-to-help-stop-the-infodemic-the-increasing-misinformation-about-coronavirus-137561
https://www.who.int/emergencies/diseases/novel-coronavirus-2019/advice-for-public/myth-busters

Chapter 6

https://www.forbesindia.com/article/thoughts/thoughts-on-being-rich/64655/1
https://theconversation.com/the-coronavirus-lockdown-is-forcing-us-to-view-screen-time-differently-thats-a-good-thing-135641
https://www.telegraph.co.uk/family/life/8-rites-passage-students-wont-get-experience-now-can-do-instead/
https://www.theguardian.com/global/2020/feb/04/tanners-tailors-and-candlestick-makers-a-history-of-apprenticeships
https://www.tes.com/news/revealed-top-100-apprenticeship-employers
https://www.theguardian.com/education/2019/apr/16/fifth-of-teachers-plan-to-leave-profession-within-two-years
https://www.century.tech/explore-century/primary-schools/
https://news.microsoft.com/en-in/features/teenager-teaching-100-teachers-minecraft/
https://en.wikipedia.org/wiki/Minecraft
https://interestingengineering.com/what-exactly-is-the-butterfly-effect#:~:text=%22The%20Butterfly%20Effect%22%20metaphor%20is,unpredictable%20by%20their%20very%20nature.
https://www.telegraph.co.uk/global-health/science-and-disease/what-r-value-means-coronavirus-lockdown-uk-rising/
https://www.mckinsey.com/featured-insights/employment-and-growth/technology-jobs-and-the-future-of-work
https://www.delltechnologies.com/content/dam/delltechnologies/assets/perspectives/2030/pdf/SR1940_IFTFforDellTechnologies_Human-Machine_070517_readerhigh-res.pdf
https://reports.weforum.org/future-of-jobs-2016/chapter-1-the-future-of-jobs-and-skills/
https://www.bbc.co.uk/bitesize/articles/zf8j92p
https://www.ey.com/en_gl/workforce/the-future-for-drivers-in-the-driverless-future
https://undutchables.nl/about-us/blog/the-eight-most-future-proof-jobs
https://www.forbes.com/sites/forbescommunicationscouncil/2020/08/19/less-is-more-why-grow-conversations-and-okrs-are-critical-for-success/?sh=1bdeda503d48
https://en.wikipedia.org/wiki/History_of_education
https://www.mooc.org/

https://www.nytimes.com/2017/07/27/upshot/switching-careers-is-hard-it-doesnt-have-to-be.html
https://blogs.lse.ac.uk/careers/2020/05/04/new-world-order/
https://www.forbes.com/sites/nextavenue/2018/02/09/the-7-transferable-skills-to-help-you-change-careers/#12aa2ba44c04

Chapter 7

https://www.theguardian.com/global/2020/jun/21/im-broken-how-anxiety-and-stress-hit-millions-in-uk-covid-19-lockdown
https://www.nhs.uk/conditions/coronavirus-covid-19/people-at-higher-risk/whos-at-higher-risk-from-coronavirus/
https://www.bbc.co.uk/programmes/articles/3G6NKRq8t04LLZLKj91cfxS/extraordinary-facts-about-the-nhs
https://www.who.int/dg/speeches/detail/who-director-general-s-opening-remarks-at-the-media-briefing-on-covid-19---1-may-2020
https://www.asthma.org.uk/advice/triggers/coronavirus-covid-19/what-should-people-with-asthma-do-now/
https://www.dailymail.co.uk/news/article-8486525/One-care-home-resident-died-minute-peak-Covid-19-crisis.html
https://techcrunch.com/2020/03/19/open-source-project-spins-up-3d-printed-ventilator-validation-prototype-in-just-one-week/
https://www.weforum.org/agenda/2020/04/10-technology-trends-coronavirus-covid19-pandemic-robotics-telehealth/
https://www.bbc.co.uk/news/health-53392148
https://www.telegraph.co.uk/global-health/science-and-disease/will-live-years-virus-expert-debilitating-after-effects-covid/
https://www.theguardian.com/commentisfree/2020/apr/17/coronavirus-discriminate-humans-racism-sexism-inequality?CMP=Share_iOSApp_Other
https://www.health.org.uk/publications/reports/the-marmot-review-10-years-on
https://papers.ssrn.com/sol3/papers.cfm?abstract_id=3618215
https://www.independent.co.uk/news/health/coronavirus-ethnic-groups-death-rate-black-males-covid-19-england-wales-a9503201.html
https://unfoundation.org/blog/post/shadow-pandemic-how-covid19-crisis-exacerbating-gender-inequality/
https://news.un.org/en/story/2020/04/1062812
https://www.cam.ac.uk/stories/digitaldivide
https://www.weforum.org/agenda/2016/07/at-the-height-of-the-cold-war-the-us-and-soviet-union-worked-together-to-eradicate-smallpox/#:~:text=Innovation-,At%20the%20height%20of%20the%20Cold%20War%2C%20the%20US%20and,of%20diplomacy%2C%20innovation%20and%20cooperation.

https://www.goodsamapp.org/NHS
https://www.creativereview.co.uk/clap-for-our-carers/
https://bmcpublichealth.biomedcentral.com/track/pdf/10.1186/s12889-020-09139-w
https://www.theguardian.com/world/2018/sep/13/workplace-gender-discrimination-remains-rife-survey-finds
https://www.mentalhealth.org.uk/a-to-z/w/work-life-balance
https://www.weforum.org/agenda/2020/08/6-ways-covid-19-will-advance-human-capital-strategies-and-governance/
https://www.independent.co.uk/life-style/health-and-families/health-news/a-stressful-workplace-could-take-33-years-off-your-life-expectancy-study-finds-a6713011.html
https://www.goodsamapp.org/
https://www.mentalhealth.org.uk/campaigns/mental-health-awareness-week/kindness-matters-guide
https://www.befriending.co.uk/news/coronavirus-09032020
https://www.gov.uk/coronavirus-volunteer-local
https://nextdoor.co.uk/
https://www.webmd.com/mental-health/news/20120731/mild-anxiety-may-shorten-persons-life#1
https://www.telegraph.co.uk/health-fitness/body/surprising-health-benefits-coronavirus-lockdown/
https://www.nhs.uk/live-well/exercise/get-running-with-couch-to-5k/

Chapter 8

https://www.forbes.com/sites/naveenjain/2013/05/04/philanthropy_as_an_entrepreneur/?sh=4c1905083c99
https://www.lovemoney.com/gallerylist/95287/ordinary-brits-raising-extraordinary-amounts-of-money-to-fight-covid19
https://www.goodwill.org/
https://www.independent.co.uk/news/health/mental-health-trusts-uk-funding-government-cuts-royal-college-psychiatrists-a8219486.html
https://charitydigital.org.uk/topics/topics/coronavirus-how-brick-and-mortar-charities-are-pivoting-service-delivery-7397
https://www.rockefellerfoundation.org/wp-content/uploads/Health-Well-being.pdf
https://www.mckinsey.com/industries/public-and-social-sector/our-insights/a-transformative-moment-for-philanthropy
https://www.weforum.org/agenda/2020/06/vaccine-development-barriers-coronavirus/
https://www.bbc.co.uk/news/business-52751661
https://www.cxooutlook.com/fighting-against-covid-19-founder-of-the-loomba-foundation-lord-raj-loomba-cbe-donates-1-lakh-surgical-face-masks-to-niti-aayog/

https://www.rockpa.org/guide/women-and-giving/
https://theconversation.com/virtual-hackathons-can-help-you-solve-coro-navirus-problems-without-leaving-your-home-136956
https://hackathon.guide/
https://digit.fyi/homeless-hackathon-series-to-kickoff-in-edinburgh/
https://www.weforum.org/agenda/2020/07/estonia-hackathon-pandem-ic-covid19-technology/
https://covid-global-hackathon.devpost.com/
https://theglobalhack.com/
https://covid19.spaceappschallenge.org/
https://www.eu-startups.com/2020/05/10-innovative-coronavirus-solu-tions-created-during-online-hackathons/
http://beautifulinformation.org/news/being-radically-open-during-the-covid-19-outbreak-covid-19-open-data-hackathon/
https://www.weforum.org/agenda/2020/03/coronavirus-and-corpo-rate-social-innovation/
https://www.bbc.com/worklife/article/20200413-how-facto-ries-change-production-to-quickly-fight-coronavirus
https://www.theargus.co.uk/news/national/uk-to-day/18438230.14-gifts-crucial-workers-coronavirus-pandemic/
https://www.entrepreneur.com/article/314679
https://thriveglobal.com/stories/immense-gratitude-immaculate-immunity/
https://www.volunteermatch.org/search?l=United%20Kingdom
https://www.mentalhealth.org.uk/blog/random-acts-kindness
https://www.moneysavingexpert.com/team-blog/2018/11/how-to-give-to-charity-for-free/
https://fundraising.co.uk/2020/03/28/how-coronavirus-is-inspiring-peo-ple-to-do-good-and-help/
https://www.gofundme.com/f/help-fight-covid19-phone-chargers-needed?utm_source=customer&utm_medium=copy_link-tip&utm_cam-paign=p_cp+share-sheet
https://blog.justgiving.com/how-to-run-your-own-virtual-community-fund-raising-event/

Chapter 9

https://www.forbes.com/sites/chetwade/2020/01/02/ceos-worry-cul-ture-holding-back-innovation/?sh=6acb792e2086
https://vinepair.com/wine-blog/interesting-drinking-customs/
https://sakasandcompany.com/winston-churchill-delegation-tips/
https://www.independent.co.uk/news/uk/home-news/its-ready-steady-go-to-a-prime-slot-for-fern-and-her-tv-chefs-1584899.html
https://www.bbc.co.uk/history/ww2peopleswar/stories/92/a1110592.shtml
https://www.stylist.co.uk/life/nostalgia-happiness-habit-lockdown-sur-vey/388308

https://www.reuters.com/article/us-health-coronavirus-britain-pubs/
ancient-british-rights-to-a-drink-in-the-pub-have-to-be-suspended-john-
son-idUSKBN21732F
https://www.bbc.co.uk/news/business-53965975
https://www.bbc.co.uk/mediacentre/latestnews/2020/coronavirus-sport
https://inews.co.uk/news/virtual-grand-national-attracts-5-million-view-
ers-nhs-coronavirus-fight-415659
https://www.catholicvoices.org.uk/survey
https://www.conservatives.com/news/coronavirus-arts-culture-package
https://www.bbc.com/future/article/20200612-how-to-help-the-world-
during-lockdown
https://www.creativeindustriesfederation.com/news/press-release-cultural-
catastrophe-over-400000-creative-jobs-could-be-lost-projected-economic
https://www.conservatives.com/news/coronavirus-arts-culture-package
https://variety.com/2017/digital/festivals/vr-ar-boost-storytell-
ing-1202407438/
https://touchingmasterpieces.com/
https://www.everymanplayhouse.com/whats-more/ghost-stories-of-the-
playhouse
https://britishmuseum.withgoogle.com/
https://discover.ticketmaster.co.uk/theatre/our-guide-to-streaming-the-
best-theatre-at-home-49832/
https://metro.co.uk/2020/08/18/17-iconic-eastenders-epi-
sodes-need-see-13121893/
https://metro.co.uk/2020/08/27/eastenders-boss-jon-sen-reveals-clever-
methods-used-cheat-social-distancing-soap-returns-13186449/
https://www.independent.co.uk/arts-entertainment/tv/news/great-british-
bake-gbbo-2020-channel-4-new-series-when-coronavirus-lockdown-matt-
lucas-a9682661.html
https://www.telegraph.co.uk/music/what-to-listen-to/will-have-reset-uk-
culture-will-take-covid-challenge/
https://www.kudos.com/
https://medium.com/@Q9ELEMENTS/are-you-a-radiator-or-a-drain-
a8646415058b
https://www.youtube.com/watch?v=wbQSAdU4Qb4
https://en.wikipedia.org/wiki/Garfield
https://theconversation.com/rural-pubs-really-do-make-countryside-com-
munities-happier-but-they-are-closing-at-an-alarming-rate-72231
https://plunkett.co.uk/more-than-a-pub/
https://www.cordonbleu.edu/news/four-ways-improve-cooking-skills/en
https://homecooking.show/
https://cooking.nytimes.com/recipes/1020830-caramelized-shallot-pasta
https://www.youtube.com/channel/UCbpMy0Fg74eXXkvxJrtEn3w
https://pastaevangelists.com/

Chapter 10

https://www.un.org/press/en/2020/sgsm20051.doc.htm
https://www.who.int/news-room/feature-stories/detail/who-manifesto-for-a-healthy-recovery-from-covid-19
https://www.who.int/about/who-we-are/constitution#:~:text=Health%20is%20a%20state%20of,belief%2C%20economic%20or%20social%20condition.
https://www.who.int/about/who-we-are/constitution#:~:text=Health%20is%20a%20state%20of,belief%2C%20economic%20or%20social%20condition.
https://www.itu.int/en/ITU-D/Statistics/Documents/facts/FactsFigures2019.pdf
https://techcabal.com/2020/05/29/africas-cloud-computing-industry-is-set-to-grow-as-data-adoption-rises/
https://www.microsoft.com/en-us/research/project/farmbeats-iot-agriculture/
https://www.nesta.org.uk/blog/smart-cities-during-covid-19/
https://www.kateraworth.com/doughnut/
https://pubmed.ncbi.nlm.nih.gov/11516376/
https://www.telegraph.co.uk/news/2020/04/19/david-attenborough-says-humanity-last-moment-save-planet-new/
https://www.who.int/news-room/feature-stories/detail/who-manifesto-for-a-healthy-recovery-from-covid-19
https://news.un.org/en/story/2020/04/1062332
https://www.theguardian.com/uk-news/2020/apr/03/uk-road-travel-falls-to-1955-levels-as-covid-19-lockdown-takes-hold-coronavirus-traffic
https://www.ons.gov.uk/economy/environmentalaccounts/articles/doesexposuretoairpollutionincreasetheriskofdyingfromthecoronaviruscovid19/2020-08-13
https://www.triplepundit.com/story/2020/could-europes-car-free-zones-become-long-term-solutions-look-three-cities-efforts/120501
https://www.theguardian.com/uk-news/2020/may/15/large-areas-of-london-to-be-made-car-free-as-lockdown-eased
https://www.businessgreen.com/news/4020416/race-zero-global-net-zero-commitments-double
https://www.weforum.org/agenda/2020/08/carbon-emission-electric-vehicles-biofuels-elctrofuels/
https://www.ons.gov.uk/employmentandlabourmarket/peopleinwork/employmentandemployeetypes/datasets/homeworkingintheuklabourmarket
https://www.theguardian.com/world/2020/sep/11/the-rule-of-six-what-are-the-new-uk-coronavirus-rules
https://www.theguardian.com/commentisfree/2020/aug/07/coronavirus-britain-sandwich-pandemic-lunchtime

https://www.theguardian.com/technology/2013/feb/25/yahoo-chief-bans-working-home
https://www.arup.com/covid-19/return-to-the-workplace
https://www.bbc.com/future/article/20200624-has-covid-19-brought-us-closer-to-stopping-climate-change
https://www.netzeroteesside.co.uk/
https://sustainability.google/commitments/
https://www.un.org/en/un-coronavirus-communications-team/un-urges-countries-%E2%80%98build-back-better%E2%80%99
https://www.vox.com/2018/10/9/17951924/climate-change-global-warming-un-ipcc-report-takeaways
https://www.nytimes.com/2020/08/24/opinion/jerry-seinfeld-new-york-coronavirus.html
https://michelleogundehin.com/happy-inside/
https://www.instagram.com/cottagenoir/?hl=en
https://www.neptune.com/furniture/home-office/desks-workstations/
https://www.ikea.com/gb/en/rooms/home-office/standing-desks-pub9712cc91
https://www.hermanmiller.com/en_gb/products/seating/office-chairs/aeron-chairs/
https://www.2ndhnd.com/
https://grillo-designs.com/
https://www.stykka.com/cardboarddesk
https://www.telegraph.co.uk/travel/comment/travel-guidebooks-coronavirus/
https://www.theguardian.com/business/2009/mar/02/mobile-phone-Internet-developing-world
https://webfoundation.org/
https://contractfortheweb.org/action/

ENDNOTES

1   www.thetimes.co.uk/article/telecity - shows-its-maverick-michael-tobin-the-door

2   https://www.oxfordlearnersdictionaries.com/definition/american_english/perfect-storm

3   https://www.gov.uk/government/speeches/pm-address-to-the-nation-on-coronavirus-23-march-2020

4   https://www.who.int/dg/speeches

5   https://www.who.int/director-general/speeches/detail/who-director-general-s-opening-remarks-at-the-media-briefing-on-covid-19--22-april-2020

6   https://www.rcpsych.ac.uk/docs/default-source/improving-care/nccmh/suicide-prevention/middle-aged-men/recession-recovery-and-suicide-in-mental-health-patients-in-england-time-trend-analy-sis---2019.pdf?sfvrsn=d6287af4_2

7   https://www.thecalmzone.net/what-we-do

8   https://www.bbc.co.uk/news/av/uk-62843295

9   https://www.linkedin.com/pulse/what-vuca-why-important-andrew-wood/

10 https://www.collinsdictionary.com/us/dictionary/english/permacrisis

11 https://journals.sagepub.com/doi/10.1177/1745691614568352

12 https://www.happiness.com/magazine/health-body/male-loneliness-time-bomb-killing-men/

13 https://www.facebook.com/ManChatAbz/

14 https://mankindproject.org/who-we-are/

15 https://www.menspeak.co.uk/

16 https://www.npr.org/sections/health-shots/2014/09/22/349875448/best-to-not-sweat-the-small-stuff-because-it-could-kill-you

17 https://todoist.com/
18 https://www.thelionsbarbercollective.com/
19 https://www.thelionsbarbercollective.com/find-locate-a-lion/
20 https://apolloneuro.com/
21 https://ouraring.com/
22 https://choosemuse.com/
23 https://www.reuters.com/world/europe/russias-putin-authorises-military-operations-donbass-domestic-media-2022-02-24/
24 https://www.collinsdictionary.com/dictionary/english/trumpism
25 https://www.who.int/news-room/spotlight/ten-threats-to-global-health-in-2019
26 https://5lovelanguages.com/
27 https://5lovelanguages.com/quizzes/love-language
28 https://getmee.ai/
29 https://www.linkedin.com/pulse/great-leaders-give-people-roots-wings-don-ledingham/
30 https://en.wikipedia.org/wiki/Great_Resignation
31 https://www.mckinsey.com/capabilities/people-and-organizational-performance/our-insights/help-your-employees-find-purpose-or-watch-them-leave
32 https://www.linkedin.com/pulse/20140805155217-28143062-if-only-i-could-fail-like-edison-and-dyson/
33 https://help.donut.ai/en/
34 https://slack.com/intl/en-gb
35 https://themagiccircle.co.uk/
36 https://founders.archives.gov/documents/Franklin/01-03-02-0130
37 https://www.vocabulary.com/dictionary/prosperity
38 https://www.thecalmzone.net/get-support
39 https://www.moneyhelper.org.uk/en
40 https://emma-app.com/
41 https://www.rescuetime.com/
42 https://www.moneysavingexpert.com/
43 https://www.stepchange.org/
44 https://www.independent.co.uk/extras/indybest/kids/joe-wicks-pe-class-home-kids-b1785287.html
45 https://www.theguardian.com/education/2019/apr/16/fifth-of-teachers-plan-to-leave-profession-within-two-years

46 https://www.entrepreneur.com/article/313349
47 https://www.playforthoughts.com/blog/steve-jobs-reality-distortion-field
48 https://envision.app/
49 https://www.telegraph.co.uk/culture/art/art-features/11153746/
The-Connor-Brothers-An-exclusive-interview.html
50 https://www.thecalmzone.net/
51 https://www.psychologytoday.com/gb/blog/the-science-behind-behav-
ior/201607/4-reasons-why-optimistic-outlook-is-good-your-health
52 https://www.goodsamapp.org/
53 https://www.volunteermatch.org/search?l=United%20Kingdom
54 https://www.princes-trust.org.uk/support-our-work/volunteer/busi-
ness-mentor
55 https://www.moneysavingexpert.com/team-blog/2018/11/how-to-
give-to-charity-for-free/
56 https://www.amazon.co.uk/What-Talk-About-When-Running/
dp/0099526158
57 https://www.nhs.uk/live-well/exercise/get-running-with-couch-to-5k/
58 https://runtogether.co.uk/get-involved/runandtalk/
59 https://thehappierapp.com/download-app
60 https://creatingthefuture.org/philanthropy-as-love-of-humanity/
61 https://hbr.org/2021/12/how-smart-tech-is-transforming-nonprofits
62 https://www.goodwill.org/
63 https://www.actionforchildren.org.uk/blog/what-is-the-extent-of-youth-
homelessness-in-the-uk/
64 https://www.nysoclib.org/blog/newton%E2%80%99s-%E2%80%9C-
year-wonders%E2%80%9D-during-great-plague
65 https://www.linkedin.com/pulse/10-tips-tricks-organize-awesome-
hackathon-mayra-castellanos/
66 https://www.wig.co.uk/what-we-offer/ned-and-trustee-recruitment/
becoming-a-nedtrustee
67 https://theheartofthecity.com/resource-hub/becoming-a-trustee-guide/
68 https://blog.feedspot.com/philanthropy_podcasts/
69 https://www.etymonline.com/word/culture
70 https://sakasandcompany.com/winston-churchill-delegation-tips/
71 https://britishheritage.com/history/britains-wwii-blitz-spirit-covid-19-
pandemic

72 https://inews.co.uk/news/virtual-grand-national-attracts-5-million-viewers-nhs-coronavirus-fight-415659

73 https://britishmuseum.withgoogle.com/

74 https://discover.ticketmaster.co.uk/theatre/our-guide-to-streaming-the-best-theatre-at-home-49832/

75 https://fablesofaesop.com/the-north-wind-and-the-sun.html

76 https://www.kudos.com/

77 https://datacentremagazine.com/data-centres/india-to-classify-data-centres-as-infrastructure

78 https://www.microsoft.com/en-us/research/project/farmbeats-iot-agriculture/

79 https://bbb-plc.com/

80 https://www.northseafarmers.org/

81 https://www.afrik21.africa/en/namibia-kelp-blue-to-develop-a-giant-kelp-farm-on-the-countrys-coasts/

82 https://www.un.org/en/climatechange/raising-ambition/renewable-energy

83 https://www.apa.org/news/press/releases/2017/03/mental-health-climate.pdf

84 https://www.headspace.com/stress/climate-anxiety

85 https://gethazelapp.com/

86 https://www.stylist.co.uk/life/careers/working-from-holiday-trend/700754s

87 https://www.cntraveler.com/story/the-best-countries-to-work-from-as-a-digital-nomad